CONTENTS

The Master Theme of the Bible

ACKNOWLEDGMENT:

It was through kindly providence that **J. Sidlow Baxter's** remarkable volume, *The Master Theme of the Bible*, first came into my hands. What began as an ordinary moment of reading soon transformed into an extraordinary encounter with truth so compelling that it would not release its hold upon my heart and mind. This first led to a series of Monday night Bible studies at George County Baptist Church, and then naturally transitioned to the book you have before you.

J. Sidlow Baxter, that faithful Australian-born servant of the Lord who blessed countless souls through his expositions of scripture, demonstrated in his comprehensive study something of great significance: the doctrine of the Lamb of God stands as the scarlet thread running through the entire fabric of Bible revelation. His careful tracing of this theme from **Genesis** to **Revelation** informed my understanding to better perceive what scripture had faithfully proclaimed all along—yet which the natural eye may fail to apprehend beneath the familiar surface of well-worn passages. As he escorts the reader from Eden's first slain sacrifice to the Lamb enthroned, scripture seems to lift its own veil: truths long resident upon the page yet curiously unseen gleam forth with sudden, grateful clarity, as though a hidden lamp had been turned toward a familiar room.

This present volume exists because of the spark that Dr. Baxter's work kindled in my soul. Where his treatment provided the broad landscape of the doctrine, I have endeavoured to offer you, dear reader, a more intimate and comprehensive pathway through that same glorious territory. My burden is not only to inform your mind about doctrinal concepts, but to introduce your heart to the Person behind the doctrine, Jesus Christ, the Lamb of God who taketh away the sin of the world.

You hold in your hands not an academic treatise (a product of which I am incapable of producing), but a personal invitation. The Lamb of God is not only a doctrine to be mastered, but, more importantly, a Saviour to be trusted. **These pages are written with the earnest prayer that you might not simply learn about the Lamb, but that you might come to know Him personally as your own Redeemer.**

DEDICATION:

This work is lovingly dedicated to three faithful servants of the Lord Jesus Christ whose devotion to Him has profoundly shaped both my ministry and my understanding of what it means to live a life wholly consecrated to our Saviour (**Romans 16:1-2**).

To Mrs. Pat Magers: Your unwavering devotion to family—tenderly caring for loved ones through every illness—and your steadfast loyalty to George County Baptist Church reflect the heart of one truly *"faithful in all things"* (**1 Timothy 3:11**). When the Lord first directed our path to this church, your immediate support revealed a soul genuinely committed to Christ and His bride. Through seasons of service and sacrifice, you have demonstrated that faithfulness which the Lord both requires and rewards, proving yourself a trustworthy steward of His grace.

To Mrs. Phillis Morgan: who is *"a succourer of many"* (**Romans 16:2**). Your faithful dedication to George County Baptist Church during its pastoral vacancy, laboring alongside Mrs. Pat to sustain the Lord's work, reveals one who serves *"not with eyeservice, as menpleasers; but as the servants of Christ"* (**Ephesians 6:6**). Whether providing comfort to those in distress or laboring alongside us in our divers ministries, you embody Christian hospitality at its best. Your generous heart toward every needy soul reflects Christ's own compassion, proving yourself a faithful steward.

To my beloved wife, Kristin: whose character embodies the very essence of the virtuous woman described in **Proverbs 31**. *"Who can find a virtuous woman?"* - I have found her! In you, my love, I have found a living demonstration of selfless devotion to Jesus Christ, to family, and to ministry. Your faithfulness to our children and to me creates the stable foundation upon which all my labors rest, pastoral or otherwise. Without your constant support, your willingness to bear the burdens of home and family, and your cheerful sacrifice of personal comfort for the sake of the gospel, I could neither work full time, study the scriptures with the diligence they require, nor write with the concentration that such work demands. You are my helper in the truest biblical sense—one who makes possible the work that God has equipped me to accomplish. Your steadfast dedication to our Saviour shines through every aspect of your daily life, and in your faithfulness I see reflected the very character of Christ Himself.

These three ladies represent *"faithful servants"*—those who labor quietly in a small town and in a small church not for earthly recognition but for the approval of their Master. May their examples inspire all who read these pages to pursue the same wholehearted devotion to the Lamb of God who gave Himself for us all.

THE FUNDAMENTAL DOCTRINE

1 Peter 1:18-21 *"Forasmuch as ye know that ye were not redeemed with corruptible things, as silver and gold, from your vain conversation received by tradition from your fathers; But with the precious blood of Christ, as of a lamb without blemish and without spot: Who verily was foreordained before the foundation of the world, but was manifest in these last times for you, Who by him do believe in God, that raised him up from the dead, and gave him glory; that your faith and hope might be in God."*

This sacred passage from the Apostle Peter's first epistle establishes the cornerstone upon which our entire study must rest. Here, at the outset of our investigation into the doctrine of the Lamb of God, we encounter the very heart of redemptive truth. These verses unveil the scarlet tapestry that scripture weaves from **Genesis** to **Revelation**, a tapestry whose central figure is Jesus Christ, the Lamb that was slain.

The careful student of scripture recognizes immediately that this passage accomplishes what no human author could devise by literary skill. It connects the temporal with the eternal, the historical with the prophetic, the Old Testament shadows with New Testament substance. That such connections emerge naturally from this sacred text, written by men separated by centuries and circumstances, testifies irrefutably to the divine inspiration that guided their pens.

THE IMMUTABLE FOUNDATION OF REDEMPTION

The Apostle Peter begins with a statement of fact that brooks no contradiction: redemption stands upon an incorruptible foundation. This declaration strikes at the very heart of man's tendency to trust in that which he can see and touch. Silver and gold, those metals which have served as measures of earthly wealth throughout human history, are dismissed as *"corruptible things"*—insufficient, temporary, and utterly inadequate for eternal redemption.

How this must have startled Peter's first readers, many of whom had spent their lives accumulating such treasures! Yet the apostle's reasoning is both sound and searching. **What use are earthly riches to the condemned soul?** What value do material possessions hold when eternal judgment looms? The very substances that men covet and hoard for security prove powerless against sin's dominion and death's sting.

This truth establishes the first fundamental principle of the doctrine of the Lamb of God: redemption must be as permanent and incorruptible as God Himself. Whatever accomplishes man's deliverance from sin must possess eternal validity, for anything less would leave the redeemed soul vulnerable to fresh condemnation. The precious blood of Christ, being godly in its source and infinite in its value, meets this immutable requirement.

THE PERFECT SACRIFICE

When Peter employs the imagery of the sacrificial lamb, he reaches back across centuries of biblical history to connect Christ's work with the entire Old Testament sacrificial system. This connection transcends simple illustration—while the sacrificial system did illuminate spiritual truths for Old Testament believers, it constituted a God-designed typology that found its ultimate fulfillment in Christ.

The lamb metaphor carries profound significance that extends far beyond poetic beauty. Under the Law of Moses, every sacrificial animal had to be examined carefully for defects. A blemished offering was not only inadequate; it was an insult to the holiness of God. The priest would scrutinize the beast, searching for any mark, wound, or imperfection that would disqualify it for sacred service.

How much more stringent must be the examination of Him who would serve as the final, perfect sacrifice? Christ's sinlessness was not only the absence of moral failure but the positive presence of absolute righteousness. He was *"without blemish"*—having no inherited corruption from Adam's fall. He was *"without spot"*—having committed no personal transgression throughout His earthly life. In Him alone would be found the perfect sacrifice that satisfied God's justice while demonstrating God's mercy.

This establishes the second fundamental principle: the Lamb's perfection was essential to His redemptive work. An imperfect savior could not save perfectly; a blemished sacrifice could not cleanse completely. Only the sinless Son of God could bear the sins of others without being consumed by the judgment those sins deserved.

THE PATIENT PLAN

Perhaps no phrase in all of scripture more fully captures the magnificent scope of God's redemptive plan than this declaration of Christ's pre-appointment to His redemptive work. This was no emergency measure hastily devised when Adam fell in Eden. This was no improvisation necessitated by unforeseen circumstances. The eternal Son was *"foreordained"* to become the Lamb of God.

The word *"foreordained"* points to God's intent and settled purpose. It indicates active predetermination regarding the Person who would be sacrificed for redemption. God did not simply know that Christ would become the sacrifice for sin; He appointed Him to that office in the council chambers of eternity. This appointment was made with full knowledge of all that it would require—the incarnation, the sinless life, the agonizing death, the glorious resurrection.

This establishes the third fundamental principle: redemption originates in the *"determinate counsel and foreknowledge of God"* (**Acts 2:22-24**), not in the temporal needs of man. While man's sin created the necessity for salvation, God's love provided the solution. Here lies a truth of grand precision: God did not choose beforehand *which souls* would receive salvation, but He most certainly appointed *which Savior* would accomplish it. This distinction should humble the proudest heart and comfort the most troubled conscience. Our salvation rests not upon man's fleeting wisdom or strength, but upon the unshakeable foundation of God's eternal plan—established not in any decree concerning individual destinies, but in the eternal appointment of Christ Jesus as *"the Lamb slain from the foundation of the world"*.

THE PRACTICAL PURPOSE

The apostle concludes this magnificent passage by revealing the practical purpose of Christ's redemptive work. It is not only to deliver man from the penalty of sin, though it surely accomplishes that blessed end. It is not limited to providing eternal life, though that precious gift is certainly included. The ultimate purpose is to establish our *"faith and hope"* in God Himself.

Here we discover the transformative power of the doctrine. When the believer truly comprehends what God has done in Christ, when he grasps the eternal planning, the perfect provision, and the complete accomplishment of redemption, his heart is drawn to trust the God who devised and executed such a plan. Faith ceases to be an intellectual exercise and becomes a settled confidence in the character and competence of the Almighty.

Hope, likewise, is anchored (**Hebrews 6:19**) not in circumstances or feelings but in the unchanging faithfulness of Him who *"raised him up from the dead, and gave him glory."* The same power that resurrected Christ from the grave stands behind every promise God has made.

This establishes the fourth fundamental principle: the doctrine of the Lamb penetrates intellectual assent to establish the very foundations of spiritual confidence. Like a master physician who diagnoses not only symptoms but the constitutional weakness beneath (**Romans 3:9-20, Romans 7:18**), this doctrine addresses the fundamental instability of the human heart. It is not enough to know truth; one must be **established** in truth.

Right doctrine leads to right living, but observe the order: doctrine must first establish the heart, and only from that established heart flows the power for godly conduct. This is no sequence of cause and effect, but rather the profound reality that **grace** itself becomes the enabling power within. *"For it is a good thing that the heart be established with grace"*—not with external observances, not with dietary regulations, not with any human contrivance, but with godly influence upon the heart which reflects itself in transformed living.

The man whose heart rests upon any other foundation—upon his own resolutions, his moral improvements, his religious activities—discovers in the moment of testing that he has built upon sand. But he who has learned to draw continually from the fountain of grace finds within himself a well of strength that runs counter to every natural inclination toward weakness and failure. This is the intensely practical nature of sound doctrine: it provides not only information for the mind, but transformation of the very seat of human action—the heart itself.

DIVINE INSPIRATION & PROGRESSIVE REVELATION

As we stand upon this foundational passage and prepare to trace the doctrine of the Lamb through scripture, we must pause to acknowledge the miraculous nature of what lies before us. The consistency with which this doctrine develops from its first shadowy appearance in **Genesis** to its glorious culmination in **Revelation** cannot be attributed to human coordination or literary genius. The biblical authors, separated by centuries, cultures, and circumstances, could never have achieved such doctrinal harmony by human effort.

Consider the mathematical impossibility of such unity: approximately **forty authors** across **fifteen centuries**, writing from three different continents in three different languages, addressing the most controversial subjects known to man—the nature of God, the meaning of existence, and the destiny of the human soul. Yet these diverse writers, from **Egyptian princes to Galilean fishermen, from warrior-kings to exiled prophets**, produced not a collection of conflicting philosophies, but a seamless tapestry of truth.

The human impossibility becomes even more striking when we consider that many of these authors **had no access to the writings of their predecessors**. How could the prophet Daniel, writing in Babylonian captivity, perfectly complement themes established by Moses a millennium earlier? How could the apostle John, penning Revelation on Patmos, bring to perfect culmination symbols and types that began in Eden? The answer lies beyond the realm of human capability.

The principle of **progressive revelation** explains this apparent phenomenon with both theological precision and pastoral comfort. God did not reveal the full truth about the Lamb of God in a single moment or through a single writer. Instead, like the master craftsman who reveals His design through stages, He chose to unfold this doctrine gradually, **like the dawn that grows brighter until the perfect day**. Each Spirit-inspired writer contributed his part to this tapestry, often without fully understanding how his contribution would fit into the larger pattern.

This progressive development serves multiple purposes, each demonstrating God's infinite wisdom in His self-disclosure:

First, it demonstrates God's authorship of scripture by displaying a consistency that transcends human ability. No human mind, however brilliant, could orchestrate such intricate harmony across millennia. When Abel offered his lamb in **Genesis 4**, when Abraham saw God's provision on Mount Moriah, when Moses instituted the Passover—each was unknowingly contributing to a grand symphony whose final movement would not be heard until the Lamb stood upon the heavenly Mount Zion. This is not human genius; this is divine orchestration.

Second, it builds anticipation and understanding gradually, like a master teacher who knows his pupils' capacity. God educated mankind in the same way a wise instructor teaches a child—beginning with simple, visible object lessons before advancing to more complex truths. The sacrificial system was not arbitrary ritual, but godly pedagogy. Each lamb slain, each altar built, each ceremony observed was preparing human hearts to recognize the ultimate sacrifice when He appeared.

Third, it provides multiple witnesses to the same truth, strengthening the believer's confidence in God's provided redemption. From **twenty-eight different references to the Lamb in Revelation alone**, to the countless Old Testament types and shadows, God surrounded this central truth with such abundant testimony that faith finds solid ground beneath its feet.

Fourth—and here we touch upon the most precious aspect of all—it reveals the **eternal nature of God's love**. The doctrine of the Lamb was not an afterthought, not a rushed response to human failure, but **the predetermined solution to an existing problem**. This progressive revelation thus becomes not only an intellectual study, but a window into the very heart of God—a heart that loved us while we were yet sinners, and provided for our redemption before we knew we needed it.

The unity of scripture stands as one of the most compelling evidences for divine inspiration. This unity is not the mechanical uniformity of human manufacture, but the organic harmony of the Holy Spirit—diverse in expression, unified in essence, perfect in its testimony to the one great theme: the Lamb of God who takes away the sin of the world.

THE PRINCIPLE OF FIRST MENTION

Our study will be guided by the established biblical principle known as the **law of first mention**. This principle recognizes that when God introduces a concept or doctrine in scripture, that initial presentation establishes the foundational understanding upon which all subsequent development builds. The first mention establishes the **DNA**, so to speak, from which the entire doctrine grows. The first mention of a given subject gives foundational keys to its subsequent understanding in other places in scripture.

Like an architect who reveals his design through the laying of the cornerstone, God establishes in each initial presentation **fundamental inherent meaning** that remains **unchangeable in the mind of God throughout scripture**. This is not human literary technique, but godly wisdom. When the Lord, who sees the end from the beginning, chooses to introduce a truth for the first time, He does so with perfect knowledge of how that truth will unfold across millennia of revelation.

Consider the implications: **Abel's sacrifice in Genesis 4:4** was not only the first recorded act of worship, but God's deliberate establishment of the spiritual genetic code for all acceptable worship that would follow.

When Moses recorded that *"the Lord had respect unto Abel and to his offering"*, he was not chronicling an isolated event, but capturing the template that would echo through every subsequent sacrifice—from the Passover lamb to the scapegoat, from the daily offerings to the ultimate offering of *"the Lamb slain from the foundation of the world"*.

This principle proves particularly valuable in tracing the Lamb of God because it prevents us from **reading later revelation back into earlier passages inappropriately**. While we understand that Abel's sacrifice points ultimately to Christ's sacrifice on Calvary, we must not impose **New Testament** doctrine upon the **Genesis** narrative in ways that violate its immediate context. The principle demands that we allow each passage to speak with its own voice, in its own time, within its own dispensational framework, even as we recognize the thread of consistency that runs through all scripture.

Yet here lies a truth of **grand precision** that separates sound biblical interpretation from the interpretive chaos that plagues erroneous Bible teaching: while the **principle of first mention** guards against reading into the text, it simultaneously **establishes the unchangeable pattern** with which any subject remains in the mind of God. The first mention of a concept is often the simplest and clearest presentation; doctrines are then more fully developed on that initial foundation. This is not human development of ideas, but godly revelation of eternal truth progressively disclosed.

The principle operates on the **fundamental concept** that controls and colors every shade of idea expressed by a term in its current usage. When we trace *"blood"* from its first mention in **Genesis 4:10** through the Levitical system to the blood of Jesus Christ, we don't find evolution of meaning, but **consistent revelation** of the same foundational truth: *"the life of the flesh is in the blood"*. The fundamental concept established in Abel's passage—that blood represents life offered in substitutionary sacrifice—never changes, though it receives **fuller explanation and richer application** as revelation proceeds.

Equally important, the principle of first mention reminds us that while doctrine develops **progressively**, it does not change **fundamentally**. This distinguishes true biblical interpretation from the theological liberalism that treats scripture as human religious development. **The basic truths established in the earliest mentions remain valid throughout scripture,** though they receive clearer articulation and broader application as the Author of our salvation progressively unfolds His word.

This understanding transforms our approach to the doctrine of the Lamb. We are not archaeologists attempting to reconstruct ancient religious concepts, but students sitting at the feet of the eternal Teacher who has arranged His curriculum with perfect wisdom. Each *"first mention"* becomes the foundational cornerstone upon which all subsequent understanding must be built.

A BIBLE-BELIEVING APPROACH

Our interpretation of scripture will rest firmly upon the **literal method** of interpretation. This approach takes the Bible at face value, understanding it to mean what it says unless the context clearly indicates otherwise. When scripture employs metaphors, symbols, or figures of speech, these are understood as literary devices designed to communicate literal truth more effectively, not to obscure it.

A WORD ABOUT OUR ENGLISH BIBLE

As a Bible-believing Christian, I approach the scriptures with full confidence in the perfection of the King James Bible as God's preserved word for the English-speaking peoples. The seventeenth-century translators worked with the theological conviction that every word of the Bible was revealed to man by God and that **the sacred text required faithful preservation without human interference.** Their *"inspired literalism"* produced a translation of such **fidelity and beauty** that it has shaped not only English Christianity, but the English language itself.

This confidence in our English Bible is not a preference or tradition—it rests upon the solid foundation that **God has promised to preserve His word.** When our Lord declared that *"Heaven and earth shall pass away, but my words shall not pass away"* (**Matthew 24:35**), He made a covenant with His people that His truth would remain accessible in every generation. I see no need whatsoever to refer to Greek or Hebrew texts when God has provided His preserved word in my own language. **Our method will not only be literal, but we will literally trust the words given us in our English Bible.**

This is not **anti-intellectual,** but rather **pro-faith.** It recognizes that *"the natural man receiveth not the things of the Spirit of God: for they are foolishness unto him: neither can he know them, because they are spiritually discerned"* (**1 Corinthians 2:14**). The same scholarship that questions the preservation of scripture in English will inevitably question its preservation in any language. We choose instead to *"walk by faith, not by sight"* (**2 Corinthians 5:7**) though ample clear evidence exists to support this pathway.

THE LITERAL METHOD EXPLAINED

The literal method stands in stark contrast to the allegorical approach that has **beset biblical interpretation throughout church history**. Rather than seeking hidden meanings beneath the surface of the text, the literal method seeks the **plain meaning** intended by the inspired author and understood by his original audience.

We take every word at its primary literal meaning unless the facts of the immediate context clearly indicate otherwise. This foundational principle protects us from the **interpretive quicksand** that has swallowed whole theological systems. The allegorical method **obscures the true meaning and legitimate application of scripture. Allegorists generally see the literal meaning of a text only as a tool for unlocking the perceived allegory.** Their pursuit of illusion causes them to ignore the truth which is actually present in the text. Wether this is done purposefully or incidentally, I cannot tell.

HOW THIS OPERATES

The allegorical method performs a kind of intellectual sleight of hand, transforming the clear declarations of revelation into cryptic riddles that require special intuition to decipher. What God intended as accessible truth becomes an esoteric puzzle, elevating the interpreter above the text itself.

LITERAL DOES NOT MEAN WOODEN

This does not mean that scripture contains no symbolic language. The Lamb imagery itself is clearly metaphorical—Christ is not literally a four-legged woolly animal. But the metaphor conveys **literal truth** about His sacrificial death and perfect character. Furthermore, that literal truth from the metaphor does not require intellectual gymnastics to recognize. The literal method simply insists that when the Bible uses symbolic language, it does so to communicate truth more vividly, not to obscure it.

True literal interpretation recognizes that God employs the full range of literary expression—from plain narrative to soaring metaphor—and honors each according to its nature. To force wooden literalism upon poetry is as destructive as imposing mystical allegory upon history. The difference lies not in **whether** we encounter figurative language, but in **how** we handle it. The literal interpreter recognizes figures of speech as **intentional literary devices** designed to communicate **specific truth** with **greater power and clarity**. The allegorical interpreter treats even plain historical narrative as **coded symbolic language** requiring **special insight** to unlock.

THE SUFFICIENCY OF OUR METHOD

This approach rests upon the bedrock conviction that scripture stands complete and sufficient for all spiritual needs. God's library is closed to expansion; no additional volumes await publication from heaven's printing press. God has spoken His final word, and that word contains everything necessary to transform lives and establish truth. When the apostle Paul said that scripture is profitable *"for doctrine, for reproof, for correction, for instruction in righteousness"* (**2 Timothy 3:16**), he was not cataloging its benefits but proclaiming its comprehensive adequacy. The Bible we hold is not a rough draft requiring scholarly revision, but the finished masterpiece of godly communication.

The literal method serves as both compass and shield—guiding us toward truth while protecting us from interpretive extremes. On one side lies the quicksand of mystical allegory, where every plain statement dissolves into spiritual symbolism; on the other stands the granite wall of academic skepticism, where revelation crumbles under the weight of human criticism. The literal approach charts a course between these hazards, requiring neither special revelation to decode hidden meanings nor advanced credentials to understand plain speech. It honors the principle that the God who created human language is perfectly capable of using it clearly, and that the Spirit of truth who guides into all truth remains the believer's most reliable guide through the word of God.

THE STUDY ROADMAP: FROM SHADOW TO SUBSTANCE

Our investigation will proceed chronologically and doctrinally through ten key passages that mark the progressive revelation of the Lamb, each building upon the foundation laid in the previous revelation:

Genesis 4 will introduce us to Abel's acceptable sacrifice, establishing that God approves only those offerings that align with His prescribed will, as demonstrated by His respect for Abel's blood sacrifice while rejecting Cain's bloodless offering.

Genesis 22 will show us Abraham's willingness to offer his *"only begotten"* son—the son of promise—foreshadowing the Father's ultimate gift of His beloved Son and establishing the principle of substitutionary provision.

Exodus 12 will present the Passover lamb, whose applied blood provided both protection from judgment and deliverance from Egyptian bondage, demonstrating that salvation requires both the shedding and the application of sacrificial blood.

The Book of Leviticus will elaborate God's comprehensive sacrificial system, revealing how the burnt offering, peace offering, sin offering, and trespass offering each prefigured distinct aspects of Christ's multifaceted redemptive work.

Isaiah 53 will provide scripture's most detailed prophetic portrait of the suffering Servant, revealing both the Lamb's voluntary anguish and His victorious accomplishment in bearing the sins of many.

John 1:29-36 will mark the pivotal transition from shadow to substance as John the Baptist publicly identifies Jesus as *"the Lamb of God which taketh away the sin of the world"*—the moment when prophecy stepped into history.

Acts 8:26-40 will demonstrate how the Ethiopian eunuch discovered the Lamb in Isaiah's ancient prophecy, illustrating how New Testament fulfillment illuminates Old Testament prediction and how the Spirit guides sincere seekers to Christ.

1 Peter 1:18-21 serves as our theological foundation, establishing that redemption requires a price beyond human ability to pay—the precious blood of Christ as the spotless Lamb foreordained before the foundation of the world.

Revelation 5 will present the glorified Lamb upon His eternal throne, worthy to open the sealed book and execute judgment because He was slain—showing how past suffering qualifies for future exaltation.

Revelation 21-22 will culminate our study in the New Jerusalem, where the Lamb reigns as both Temple and Light of the eternal city, demonstrating that God's redemptive plan finds its ultimate expression in the Lamb's eternal glory.

THE DUAL PURPOSE

This study serves a dual purpose that reflects both the precision of sound doctrine and the passion of devoted discipleship. Like a physician who must first diagnose accurately before he can prescribe effectively, we seek first to establish our understanding upon the foundation of biblical truth. God has not abandoned us to the intellectual chaos that characterizes our age—that peculiar modern malady where every man becomes his own theologian and every opinion masquerades as revelation. He has spoken with surgical precision in His preserved word, and careful study will anchor our souls in godly certainty rather than the shifting sands of theological fashion. When the Great Physician has provided His complete diagnosis and prescription, we need not consult those who peddle spiritual remedies from the laboratories of human imagination.

Yet here lies the supreme danger that has shipwrecked countless souls upon the rocks of religious formalism: knowledge alone, however orthodox and extensive, cannot heal the deep disease of spiritual indifference. The scholar who accumulates biblical facts as a miser hoards coins has missed the point entirely. *"Knowledge puffeth up, but charity edifieth"* (**1 Corinthians 8:1**). The apostle's warning cuts like a scalpel to the heart of our condition—that we might become connoisseurs who have lost the capacity for wonder, biblical experts who can dissect truth but never digest it.

The second and supremely vital purpose of our study is to kindle and deepen our love for the Lamb who was slain for us. This is not sentiment, but the most practical of all objectives. As we trace His progressive revelation through scripture, as we discover how every sacrifice pointed with trembling finger toward His coming sacrifice, as we begin to fathom the infinite ocean of His redemptive love, something sacred should happen within the secret chambers of the heart. *"And they said one to another, Did not our heart burn within us, while he talked with us by the way, and while he opened to us the scriptures?"* (**Luke 24:32**).

Observe the pattern: Christ opened the scriptures, and hearts became furnaces of holy affection. The same blessed Savior who unfolded the mysteries of His Person from Moses and all the prophets desires to set our souls ablaze as He reveals Himself as the Lamb of God throughout the word of God. True biblical study should leave us not only informed but transformed, not simply educated but sanctified, not just enlightened but enraptured.

This marriage of sound doctrine and fervent devotion reflects the very nature of saving faith itself. Faith worthy of the name is never content to inhabit the cold corridors of intellectual assent, though it certainly begins there. Like a river that must have both banks to flow with power, genuine faith requires both the solid embankment of truth and the living current of love. It engages the complete person—mind enlightened by revelation, heart kindled by grace, and will surrendered in joyful obedience.

Our study must therefore accomplish this threefold work: inform our minds with the glory of the Lamb's person, warm our hearts with the wonder of His love, and compel our wills toward devoted service in His cause. For the heart that truly beholds Jesus as the Lamb of God—that sees Him both in His humiliation and His exaltation, both in His suffering and His glory—such a heart cannot remain unmoved. *"If ye love me, keep my commandments"* (**John 14:15**). Here is love proven not by profession but by practice, not by emotion but by devotion, not by feeling but by following.

FROM SACRIFICE TO GLORY

The doctrine of the Lamb of God encompasses the entire arc of redemptive history. It begins with the tragic necessity created by man's sin and concludes with the eternal glory that redemption secures. It reveals both the depths of man's sin and the heights of God's love. It demonstrates both the justice that demands satisfaction and the mercy that provides it.

As we trace this doctrine through scripture, we will witness the gradual unveiling of God's redemptive plan. We will see how each revelation adds clarity to the picture while maintaining perfect consistency with all that has gone before. We will discover that every sacrifice in the Old Testament was a promissory note, as it were, written against the account of the Lamb who was to come.

Most notably, we will see how this doctrine, which begins with the sorrows of sacrifice, culminates in the songs of the redeemed. The Lamb who was slain becomes the Lamb upon the throne. The One who bore our griefs and carried our sorrows becomes the source of eternal joy and the subject of endless praise.

The journey from sacrifice to glory is the journey of redemption itself. It is the journey that every believer travels, from the recognition of sin and judgment to the enjoyment of salvation and security. It is the journey that reveals both the terrible cost of sin and the infinite value of the soul that God was willing to redeem at such a price.

I pray this study serves to deepen your understanding of what God has done for you in Christ, and may that understanding kindle in your heart an ever-brighter flame of love and devotion to the Lamb of God who taketh away the sin of the world.

Thomas Irvin
George County Baptist Church
www.georgecountybaptistchurch.com
Lucedale, Mississippi

CHAPTER ONE

The First Blood Sacrifice

Genesis 4 will introduce us to Abel's acceptable sacrifice, establishing that God approves only those offerings that align with His prescribed will, as demonstrated by His respect for Abel's blood sacrifice while rejecting Cain's bloodless offering.

THE FUNDAMENTALS OF WORSHIP

GENESIS 4:1-7 "*AND ADAM knew Eve his wife; and she conceived, and bare Cain, and said, I have gotten a man from the LORD. And she again bare his brother Abel. And Abel was a keeper of sheep, but Cain was a tiller of the ground. And in process of time it came to pass, that Cain brought of the fruit of the ground an offering unto the LORD. And Abel, he also brought of the firstlings of his flock and of the fat thereof. And the LORD had respect unto Abel and to his offering: But unto Cain and to his offering he had not respect. And Cain was very wroth, and his countenance fell. And the LORD said unto Cain, Why art thou wroth? and why is thy countenance fallen? If thou doest well, shalt thou not be accepted? and if thou doest not well, sin lieth at the door. And unto thee shall be his desire, and thou shalt rule over him.*"

This passage provides us with the account of the first recorded worship service after man's fall into sin. Here, in these seven verses, we encounter the establishment of fundamental principles that would govern acceptable worship throughout all subsequent revelation. Through the contrasting sacrifices of Cain and Abel, we learn profound truths about blood atonement and see the first foreshadowing of Christ as the ultimate sacrificial Lamb.

Here, in this solemn account, the thoughtful reader discerns a narrative whose profound simplicity is of godly origin. It is here that the Lord engraves into the bedrock of human history the unalterable laws of spiritual approach: that fellowship with a holy God is not earned by the sincere toil of a man's own hand, but is granted only through the substitutionary shedding of blood, a lesson first demonstrated by God Himself at Eden's mandatory exit. By faith, Abel grasped this revealed truth and brought a living sacrifice, thereby becoming the first in a long line of witnesses to the necessity of a blood atonement. In this single act, a pattern is set, a doctrine is established, and a scarlet thread is woven that will run through all the ages, finding its glorious and final consummation in the Lamb which taketh away the sin of the world.

THE DIVINE PATTERN ESTABLISHED

The narrative begins with the birth of the first generation born into a fallen world, introducing us to Abel, whose very name means *"breath"* or *"vanity,"* reminding us of the frailty of human life in a sin-cursed world (James 4:14). Yet this brief life would establish eternal principles that guide worship until the end of time. Abel's role as a keeper of sheep connects him immediately to the broader biblical theme of shepherding that culminates in Christ as the Good Shepherd who lays down His life for His sheep.

Genesis 4 reveals that Cain and Abel already knew that God demands sacrifice, for *"in process of time"* marks this as a commanded, recurring observance rather than a spontaneous impulse. Here, within humanity's first chapter of exile from Eden, worship emerges not as haphazard fervor but as disciplined, instructed devotion—an organized approach to the true and living God. This understanding may have originated from God's first sacrifice in **Genesis 3:21**: *"Unto Adam also and to his wife did the LORD God make coats of skins, and clothed them."* When God clothed Adam and Eve with animal skins, He established the foundational principle that sin requires covering through the shedding of blood. This example would have instructed their children about proper approaches to worship.

THE CONTRAST OF HEART AND OFFERING

In the account of Cain and Abel's offerings, we uncover **essential principles** that undergird all acceptable worship before God. Cain brought *"of the fruit of the ground"*—an offering of honest labor, but one utterly devoid of blood. The scriptures, revealing the necessity of blood atonement, make it clear that such an offering could never suffice: *"Without shedding of blood is no remission"* (**Hebrews 9:22**). Cain's act, while reflecting sincerity, tragically misunderstands the very foundation of communion with a holy God. **No matter how sincere or diligent, human effort alone cannot bridge the chasm created by sin.**

By contrast, Abel's offering embodies three **profound, God-revealed elements** that foreshadow true worship and point toward Christ, the Lamb of God:

Blood: Abel brought a living sacrifice—blood was shed, and life was laid down. This echoes the principle taught in **Leviticus 17:11**: *"For the life of the flesh is in the blood: and I have given it to you upon the altar to make an atonement for your souls."* Here is the sacred transaction: life for life, sacrifice for sin. **Only blood can satisfy the requirement of God's justice against sin.**

Firstlings: Abel presented the firstborn of his flock, not the leftovers or the surplus, but the prime, the beginning of his increase. This act of giving the best, the first, is a principle repeated throughout scripture—from the dedication of the firstborn (**Exodus 13:2**) to the call to honor God with the firstfruits of all our increase (**Proverbs 3:9**). **God's claim upon the first and best is a perpetual reminder that He must have preeminence.**

Fat: Abel included *"the fat thereof"*—the choicest, richest portion, reserved in later sacrificial worship for God alone (**Leviticus 3:16**). **This signifies not just giving, but giving with excellence, offering to God what is most precious, most valuable, most pleasing.**

Worship—true worship—is never a matter of ritual, nor is it the offering of convenient surplus. **It is the surrender of life, the yielding of the best, and the presentation of all that is most costly, motivated by faith and love.** As **Hebrews 11:4** affirms, *"By faith Abel offered unto God a more excellent sacrifice than Cain."* The difference was not in the act alone, but in the heart: Abel approached God in faith, while Cain's offering, though outwardly respectable, lacked the response of obedient trust.

Thus, the passage lays the foundation for a doctrine of worship that reaches its climax in the cross. **God's acceptance is never purchased by human merit or ingenuity, but is only granted through a substitutionary sacrifice—one that Abel's lamb foreshadowed, but which Christ alone fulfilled.** This lesson is not only historical, but deeply practical: the heart that grasps the true pattern of worship will seek not to impress God with its own righteousness, but to trust in the Lamb that God has provided.

As the book unfolds, these principles will reappear, each progressive revelation adding clarity and depth to the doctrine of the Lamb. **Cain's offering was rejected for want of blood and obedience; Abel's was accepted by grace through faith—a pattern which, in the fullness of time, will find its perfect expression in the cross of Christ.** Let us, therefore, approach God not with the fruit of our own hands alone, but through the once-for-all sacrifice of the Lamb of God, who takes away the sin of the world.

GOD'S EVALUATION AND APPROVAL

The scriptures record with stark clarity: "*And the LORD had respect unto Abel and to his offering: but unto Cain and to his offering he had not respect.*" Here, the phrase "*had respect unto*" indicates God's favorable approval and acceptance—He welcomed Abel's offering but decidedly rejected Cain's.

This decisive judgment demonstrates that God evaluates not only the outward act of worship, but also the heart and faith from which worship springs. As **Hebrews 11:4** explains: *"By faith Abel offered unto God a more excellent sacrifice than Cain..."* The difference was not in the sincerity of their human intentions, but in the presence or absence of faith responding to God's revealed expectations. **Romans 10:17** further confirms: *"So then faith cometh by hearing, and hearing by the word of God."* True worship must be shaped by God's word, not by human imagination.

The foundation for this approach to worship is laid bare in **Genesis 3:21**, where God Himself provided animal skins to cover Adam and Eve's sin. God's initiative in blood sacrifice set the pattern—atonement, even in mankind's earliest days, necessitated the shedding of blood. Cain's bloodless offering, however sincere, represented a tragic innovation. It anticipated the recurring human error of seeking acceptance before God through works, tradition, or religion rather than through His prescribed way.

Scripture later issues a sobering warning against *"the way of Cain"* (**Jude 1:11**)—the path of self-justifying worship, marked by rebellion and the rejection of God's authority. Abel's sacrifice, by contrast, was both a confession of faith and a prophetic sign: the *"firstlings of the flock and of the fat thereof"* pointed forward to the Lamb of God, who would one day offer Himself as the perfect, sufficient atonement for sin.

This passage stands as a perpetual call to true worship. It teaches us that God honors only that worship which is offered in the obedience of faith, according to His revealed word, and in humble gratitude for the Lamb He has provided. All who heed this biblical pattern avoid the *"way of Cain"* and find acceptance, not by their own merits, but by what God Himself has accomplished through His Son.

THE PROGRESSIVE REVELATION OF THE LAMB

Abel's acceptable sacrifice establishes **the cornerstone principle** upon which all subsequent revelation of the Lamb will build: **God alone determines the conditions of acceptable worship**. While later chapters will reveal the richness and complexity of sacrificial typology, this foundational account provides the essential framework—blood must be shed, the best must be offered, and faith must guide the worshiper's approach.

What makes this revelation particularly significant is its **stark simplicity**. Unlike the elaborate ceremonies that would follow in the Mosaic system, Abel's sacrifice demonstrates that the heart of acceptable worship lies not in ritual complexity but in humble obedience to God's prescription. This creates the doctrinal foundation upon which the entire sacrificial system would be erected.

The narrative's power lies in what it **establishes rather than explains**. Abel's sacrifice does not reveal the full meaning of substitutionary atonement—that understanding would unfold gradually through subsequent revelation. Instead, it establishes the **immutable principle** that fellowship with God requires the shedding of blood and the response of faith.

This chapter thus serves as the **doctrinal cornerstone** for all that follows. Every future sacrifice, from the Passover lamb to the scapegoat, from the daily offerings to the ultimate offering of Christ Himself, will validate and fulfill the pattern first demonstrated in Abel's acceptable worship. The progressive nature of revelation ensures that while the meaning deepens, the foundation never shifts.

FAITH, OBEDIENCE, AND THE HEART OF WORSHIP

Abel's faith manifested in his willingness to sacrifice the best of his flock, demonstrating his understanding that true worship involves giving God our finest, not our convenience. This faith-filled sacrifice makes Abel the first in Scripture's Hall of Faith (**Hebrews 11**) and establishes that acceptable worship has always been a matter of faith expressed through obedience to God's word.

This establishes the third fundamental principle: true worship must be offered in faith and according to God's revealed pattern. Abel's sacrifice looked forward through faith to the ultimate sacrifice that God would provide in His own Son. Though he could not have understood the full implications of his act, Abel established the truth that would echo throughout scripture: *"without shedding of blood is no remission"* (**Hebrews 9:22**).

CAIN'S TRAGIC EXAMPLE AND ITS MODERN PARALLELS

Cain's bloodless offering stands as a solemn warning against presumptuous worship. In bringing *"of the fruit of the ground,"* he usurped God's prerogative to prescribe the terms of communion, omitting the very element—blood—upon which atonement and acceptance depend. When God *"had not respect unto Cain and to his offering,"* Cain's reaction exposed the heart of presumption: *"Cain was very wroth, and his countenance fell"* (**Genesis 4:5**). Instead of humbly realigning his worship with God's instruction, he hardened his heart and blamed God.

This initial act of disobedience set Cain on a downward spiral. His refusal to accept correction led to bitterness, alienation, and ultimately fratricide. As scripture records, "*Wherefore slew he him? because his own works were evil, and his brother's righteous*" (**1 John 3:12**). Cain's horror teaches us that presumption in worship not only severs fellowship with God but fractures relationships with those who remain faithful.

Modern parallels abound wherever individuals or communities craft worship and morality by personal preference rather than by God's revealed word. This error fuels spiritual anxiety, moral confusion, and division—symptoms not unlike the world's current mental health crises and political polarization. When people refuse God's prescription and demand to set their own terms, they sow the seeds of alienation and hostility. This will ultimately result in harm, at some level, to the persons who diligently obey God's word.

By contrast, Abel's humble obedience—offering the blood of the firstlings and the fat thereof in faith—stands as the enduring example. His sacrifice rebukes all presumptuous worship and invites us to approach God only in the way He has ordained, lest we, like Cain, reap the bitter harvest of rebellion.

Let this ancient tragedy serve as a timeless admonition: true worship requires humble submission to God's revealed will. Any attempt to worship on personal terms is not only insufficient—it is a path that leads away from God's presence and toward judgment.

THE ENDURING FOUNDATION

Though Abel suffered martyrdom, his faithful obedience secured eternal reward and an enduring testimony that "*yet speaketh*" throughout scripture. His sacrifice continues to proclaim the necessity of approaching God through faith and according to His word. Abel's example teaches that obedience to God's instructions, even when costly, brings God's approval and creates a legacy transcending temporal circumstances.

The account of Cain and Abel's offerings establishes fundamental principles regarding acceptable worship: sin requires blood atonement, God determines acceptable worship, and our approach must be characterized by faith-filled obedience rather than self-determined offerings. This early sacrifice forms the first link in scripture's progressive revelation of the Lamb of God, demonstrating that the Bible presents a unified message about redemption through blood sacrifice from beginning to end.

This establishes the fourth fundamental principle: approach to God has always required faith, obedience, and acknowledgment that fellowship with God is possible only through the blood of the Lamb. Abel's faithful example thus serves as the foundational presentation of truths that culminate in the gospel itself, proving once again that scripture is about Christ from **Genesis** to **Revelation**.

CHAPTER TWO

ABRAHAM'S OFFERING AND GOD'S PROVISION

Genesis 22 will show us Abraham's willingness to offer his *"only begotten"* son—the son of promise—foreshadowing the Father's ultimate gift of His beloved Son and establishing the principle of substitutionary provision.

THE SUPREME TEST OF FAITH

GENESIS 22:1-2 *"AND IT came to pass after these things, that God did tempt Abraham, and said unto him, Abraham: and he said, Behold, here I am. And he said, Take now thy son, thine only son Isaac, whom thou lovest, and get thee into the land of Moriah; and offer him there for a burnt offering upon one of the mountains which I will tell thee of."*

In **Genesis 22**, the doctrine of the Lamb of God moves from Abel's worshipful obedience to a profound display of godly willingness. Whereas Abel simply obeyed God's prescription for sacrifice, here God Himself orchestrates a scenario in which Abraham must offer his beloved son. This narrative not only underscores the necessity of blood atonement but advances the revelation by showing that **God Himself pro-**

vides the substitute—anticipating the Father's provision of His only begotten Son at Calvary.

The narrative commences with a statement that strikes at the very heart of comfortable religion: "*And it came to pass after these things, that God did tempt Abraham.*" The word "*tempt*" carries the meaning of testing or proving, rather than enticing to sin. This was not Satan's work but God's examination, designed not to destroy Abraham's faith but to reveal its quality and strength. Charles Spurgeon once observed, "*Strong faith is often exercised with strong trials, and put upon hard services*".

God's command was calculated to produce maximum anguish: "*Take now thy son,* **thine only son Isaac,** **whom thou lovest,** *and get thee into the land of Moriah; and offer him there for a burnt offering upon one of the mountains which I will tell thee of.*" Each phrase was like a dagger thrust into Abraham's heart. Notice the deliberate progression: "*thy son*"—not a servant or animal from his herds; "*thine only son*"—the unique heir of promise; "*Isaac*"—named specifically to remove any possibility of confusion; "*whom thou lovest*"—emphasizing the precious relationship that would be severed.

This threefold description, "*thy son, thine only son Isaac, whom thou lovest*" provides a startling parallel to the Father's relationship with Jesus Christ. Scripture declares that Jesus is God's "*only begotten Son*" **(John 3:16)** whom the Father loves. The language is not coincidental but prophetic, pointing forward to that greater sacrifice when the heavenly Father would offer His beloved Son for the sins of the world.

ABRAHAM'S COMPLETE OBEDIENCE

The patriarch's response reveals the depth of genuine faith under extreme testing. *"And Abraham rose up early in the morning, and saddled his ass, and took two of his young men with him, and Isaac his son, and clave the wood for the burnt offering, and rose up, and went unto the place of which God had told him."* There was no argument with God, no lengthy deliberation with flesh and blood, no consultation with Sarah about this heart-rending command.

Abraham's obedience demonstrates certain crucial elements of mature faith:

First, he recognized the voice of God and submitted to His authority without reservation.

Second, he prepared methodically for the sacrifice, even cutting the wood that would consume his son, a detail that reveals the completeness of his surrender to God's will.

Third, he acted decisively, rising early the next morning rather than postponing the inevitable.

Upon reaching the appointed place, Abraham demonstrated complete submission to God's command: *"And Abraham built an altar there, and laid the wood in order, and bound Isaac his son, and laid him on the altar upon the wood. And Abraham stretched forth his hand, and took the knife to slay his son."* This moment represents the pinnacle of human faith under God's testing. Abraham's willingness to proceed with the sacrifice reveals his absolute trust in God's character and promises.

This immediate compliance stands in stark contrast to the prolonged negotiations that characterize much contemporary Christianity. When God commands believers today to "*love not the world,*" they frequently respond with charges of legalism and extremism. Yet Abraham, faced with a command infinitely more difficult to accept, demonstrated unwavering obedience that has become the standard for all who would walk by faith.

Obedience to God's word is the unchanging duty of every believer, for God's commands flow from infinite wisdom and perfect love. Scripture teaches that "*without faith it is impossible to please him*" (**Hebrews 11:6**), and faith without works is dead (**James 2:17**). When we obey before fully understanding, we demonstrate trust in God's character and His promises. Thus, obedience is not only a duty but our highest privilege: it positions us to receive God's blessing, affirms our confidence in God's word, and conforms our hearts to the likeness of Christ, whose own obedience unto death secured our redemption (**Philippians 2:8**).

A TYPE OF DEATH AND RESURRECTION

"*Then on the third day Abraham lifted up his eyes, and saw the place afar off.*" The three-day journey to Moriah was both geographical necessity and doctrinal symbol. During these three days, Abraham carried within his heart the burden of anticipated grief, yet maintained his confidence in God's ultimate faithfulness. As the writer of Hebrews explains, Abraham reasoned that God was able to raise Isaac from the dead, believing that somehow both he and his son would return from this journey.

The three-day motif appears throughout scripture as a symbol of God's intervention and resurrection power. **Moses** requested a three-day journey into the wilderness for Israel to sacrifice to the Lord. **Jonah** spent three days in the belly of the great fish before being delivered. Most significantly, **Christ** would spend three days in the tomb before His resurrection. Thus Abraham's three-day journey to Moriah foreshadows the three days that would elapse between Christ's death and resurrection.

When Abraham instructed his servants to *"Abide ye here with the ass; and I and the lad will go yonder and worship, **and come again to you**,"* he demonstrated remarkable faith by his confidence that they would return together. His expectation that both he and Isaac would return reveals his confidence that God would fulfill His promises concerning Isaac, even if that required resurrection from the dead.

HEAVEN'S INTERVENTION AND SUBSTITUTIONARY SAC-RIFICE

At the critical moment when Abraham's knife was raised to slay his son, God's intervention prevented the completion of the sacrifice: *"And the angel of the LORD called unto him out of heaven, and said, Abraham, Abraham: and he said, Here am I. And he said, Lay not thine hand upon the lad, neither do thou any thing unto him: for now I know that thou fearest God, seeing thou hast not withheld thy son, thine only son from me."*

The repetition of Abraham's name communicates the urgency of heaven's intervention. God's commendation—*"now I know that thou fearest God"*—was a public declaration of the proven quality of Abraham's faith. The test was complete; Abraham had demonstrated his willingness to surrender even his most precious possession in obedience to God's command.

Immediately after the angel's intervention, Abraham discovered God's provision: *"And Abraham lifted up his eyes, and looked, and behold behind him a ram caught in a thicket by his horns: and Abraham went and took the ram, and offered him up for a burnt offering in the stead of his son."* The phrase *"in the stead of his son"* contains the essential principle of substitutionary atonement. The ram died in Isaac's place, just as Christ would later die in our place.

This ram, caught in a thicket by its horns, provides a remarkable prefigurement of Christ crowned with thorns. The substitute was not originally intended (Isaac was), but became the God-provided offering. Similarly, humanity was destined for death because of sin, but Christ became our substitute, bearing our punishment and dying in our place. As **Isaiah** prophesied, *"All we like sheep have gone astray; we have turned every one to his own way; and the LORD hath laid on him the iniquity of us all"* (**Isaiah 53:6**).

JEHOVAH-JIREH

The names men give to places in the extremity of trial are rarely trivial; they are monuments of the soul, inscriptions of a truth learned in the crucible of anguish or deliverance. Of all such names, none echoes with more tender and awful significance than **Jehovah-Jireh**, *"the LORD will provide,"* a declaration that rises from the desolate peak of Mount Moriah to sound a note of hope throughout the ages. This naming was no simple commemoration of a fortunate escape, but a prophetic act whose full meaning would only be disclosed through the slow unfolding of redemptive history.

One must contemplate the sacred geography wherein the great movements of God converge. It was no accident of terrain that this same peak, Moriah, was where centuries later, *"Solomon began to build the house of the LORD"* (**2 Chronicles 3:1**). The ground that once bore the weight of a father's agony would one day bear the edifice of a nation's worship. This convergence reveals not a series of disconnected events, but a single, deliberate design prepared for the drama of redemptive history.

The narrative itself is a study in sublime and terrible faith. We pause before the simple, piercing query of Isaac: *"Behold the fire and the wood: but where is the lamb for a burnt offering?"* It is a question of innocent logic that lays bare the horrifying reality of the moment. Abraham's reply, *"My son, God will provide himself a lamb for a burnt offering,"* is therefore not a desperate evasion but a staggering prophecy, a truth wrested from the very jaws of despair. The immediate provision of the ram caught in the thicket was the seal upon his faith, yet it pointed beyond itself to a final and more perfect sacrifice.

In this memorial, the character of God's provision is made plain. We first perceive its **unerring foresight**, for the ram was already entangled in the thicket, an answer prepared before the crisis had reached its dreadful climax. God's solution was in place before the petition was fully formed. We then witness its **awful precision**, for the angel of the LORD intervenes at that final, unbearable instant when the knife is raised. His help is never premature, lest we fail to learn our utter dependence, nor is it tardy, lest we fall into despair. Finally, we apprehend its **perfect sufficiency**. The ram was an adequate substitute for Isaac, a life for a life, prefiguring the Lamb of God, Jesus Christ, who is the all-sufficient sacrifice for the sin of the world.

The final pronouncement—"*And Abraham called the name of that place Jehovah-jireh: as it is said to this day, In the mount of the LORD it shall be seen*"—carries a weight that its speaker could only dimly have grasped. What was "*seen*" on Moriah that day was a shadow: God's willingness to provide a substitute to spare a single beloved son. What would be "*seen*" centuries later upon that same ridge of hills, at a place called Calvary, was the substance: **God's provision of Himself as the ultimate substitute for the salvation of all humanity**.

Therefore, Mount Moriah stands as an everlasting testimony that God's redemptive plan is not a frantic reaction to human failure, but a deliberate unfolding of purpose. The God who furnished a temporal remedy for the patriarch is the very God who also provides the eternal solution, His own Son. His promises are thus written into the very geography of His work, offering to every burdened soul the quiet and settled confidence that He who sees the end from the beginning will surely provide.

SILENCE AT CALVARY

The profound contrast between Abraham's experience and the Father's sacrifice of Christ lies in heaven's response. For Isaac, the voice of God interrupted the sacrifice and provided a substitute. For Jesus, heaven remained silent as He bore the sins of the world. This silence was necessary for our salvation—had God intervened to save Jesus as He saved Isaac, the plan of redemption would have remained incomplete.

The silence of heaven during Christ's crucifixion was not abandonment but accomplishment (**Luke 9:28-31**). "*Yet it pleased the LORD to bruise him... He shall see of the travail of his soul, and shall be satisfied... for he shall bear their iniquities.*" (**Isaiah 53:10-11**). For Abraham, the

Lord was pleased by his obedience and intervened, for Christ the Father was pleased by His obedience but remained silent until the sacrifice was complete.

ABRAHAM AS A TYPE OF GOD THE FATHER

Throughout this narrative, Abraham serves as a remarkable type of God the Father. As the *"father of the faithful,"* Abraham represents the heavenly Father's giving character and action in the plan of redemption. Both are fathers who love their sons deeply yet are willing to sacrifice them for a greater purpose. Both journey to the place of sacrifice fully anticipating that they would give their sons.

The parallels between Abraham and the Father extend to the testing itself. Just as Abraham's faith was proven through his willingness to offer Isaac, the Father's love for fallen man was demonstrated through His willingness to offer Christ. The difference lies in the completion of the sacrifice—Abraham was spared the ultimate anguish, but the Father was not.

ISAAC AS A TYPE OF CHRIST

"As they ascended the mountain, Abraham laid the wood of the burnt offering upon Isaac his son; and he took the fire in his hand, and a knife; and they went both of them together" (**Genesis 22:6**). In this silent cooperation, Isaac—though unaware of the full gravity—illustrates **a willing submission** that prefigures Christ's own resolve: *"Lo, I come to do thy will, O God"* (**Hebrews 10:7**). His unhesitating carriage of the wood models the posture of a true servant: humble, obedient, and entirely yielded to his Father's command.

Isaac's role provides a striking prefigurement of Christ's redemptive work through both **parallels** and **contrasts**. Both are beloved sons of their fathers, both are heirs of significant promises, and both submit willingly to their fathers' plans. Isaac carries the wood for his sacrifice just as Christ carried His cross to Calvary. When Isaac innocently asked, *"Behold the fire and the wood: but where is the lamb for a burnt offering?"* (**Genesis 22:7**), his question points forward to Christ as the ultimate Lamb of God, while Abraham's faith-filled response—*"My son, God will provide himself a lamb for a burnt offering"* (**Genesis 22:8**)—underscores that God, not man, would supply the sacrifice.

The account of Isaac on Moriah is a masterclass in doctrinal foreshadowing, yet its power is magnified most intensely in the points where the comparison breaks down. The differences do not diminish the typology; they fulfill it. Isaac, the beloved son, was ultimately spared—a ram caught in the thicket became his substitute, demonstrating God's provision in the face of death. But Christ, the beloved Son, was not spared, for He Himself was the provision. The drama on Moriah ends with a release from sacrifice; the drama on Calvary ends with the completion of it.

Furthermore, Isaac's role was one of passive, perhaps unknowing, submission. Christ's was one of active, resolute obedience. He did not simply acquiesce to His fate; He set His face like a flint toward Jerusalem, fully aware of the *"contradiction of sinners against himself"* that awaited Him (**Hebrews 12:2-3**). Where Isaac was bound by ropes, Christ was bound by love.

THE PROGRESSIVE REVELATION CONTINUES

Abraham's sacrifice of Isaac represents a crucial development in the progressive revelation of the Lamb of God. Building upon the foundation laid by Abel's acceptable sacrifice, this account adds the dimensions of God's provision, substitutionary atonement, and the costliness of redemption. The elements present in this narrative—the father's willing sacrifice of his beloved son, the son's submissive cooperation, and God's provision of a substitute—would all find their fulfillment in Christ's redemptive work.

This establishes the fifth fundamental principle of the doctrine of the Lamb: redemption requires the Father's willingness to sacrifice what is most precious to Him. Abraham's readiness to offer Isaac foreshadows the heavenly Father's actual offering of His only begotten Son. The earthly father was spared the ultimate sacrifice; the heavenly Father was not.

The sixth fundamental principle emerges from Isaac's cooperation: redemption requires the Son's willing submission to the Father's plan. Isaac's submission to being bound and placed upon the altar prefigures Christ's voluntary surrender to crucifixion. As Jesus declared, *"Therefore doth my Father love me, because I lay down my life, that I might take it again. No man taketh it from me, but I lay it down of myself"* (**John 10:17-18**).

This encounter on Moriah therefore codifies key truths that govern the doctrine of redemption:

First, acceptable sacrifice must be costly—it must represent the surrender of what is most precious.

Second, God Himself must provide the sacrifice for sin. Abraham's declaration that "*God will provide himself a lamb*" proves prophetic beyond his understanding.

Third, it establishes the principle of substitutionary atonement—the ram died "*in the stead of*" Isaac, pointing forward to Christ's death for sinners.

THE FOUNDATION FOR FUTURE REVELATION

This passage establishes crucial foundations upon which all subsequent revelation concerning the Lamb of God would build. The Passover lamb in **Exodus**, the elaborate sacrificial system in **Leviticus**, the suffering servant in **Isaiah**, and the Lamb of God in the **New Testament** all find their anticipation in the drama enacted on Mount Moriah. Abraham's prophetic declaration that "*God will provide himself a lamb*" would echo through the corridors of redemptive history until it found its fulfillment in Christ.

As we continue our study of the Lamb of God through scripture, we must remember that Abraham's experience at Moriah provides the template for understanding God's redemptive work. Every subsequent sacrifice, every offering prescribed in the law, every prophetic announcement of coming redemption finds its interpretive key in the truths established on that mountain where God proved He would indeed provide Himself as the Lamb for an offering. The father of the faithful (**Romans 4:16, Galatians 3:6-9**) has shown us the heart of the heavenly Father, and in that revelation we discover both the necessity and the certainty of our redemption through the Lamb that was slain.

CHAPTER THREE

THE PASSOVER—JUDGMENT AND DELIVERANCE

Exodus 12 will present the Passover lamb, whose applied blood provided both protection from judgment and deliverance from Egyptian bondage, demonstrating that salvation requires both the shedding and the application of sacrificial blood.

EGYPT'S MIDNIGHT HOUR

EXODUS 12:1-4 *"AND THE LORD spake unto Moses and Aaron in the land of Egypt, saying, This month shall be unto you the beginning of months: it shall be the first month of the year to you. Speak ye unto all the congregation of Israel, saying, In the tenth day of this month they shall take to them every man a lamb, according to the house of their fathers, a lamb for an house: And if the household be too little for the lamb, let him and his neighbour next unto his house take it according to the number of the souls; every man according to his eating shall make your count for the lamb."*

Exodus 12 opens upon a scene of impending doom and deliverance. Egypt, once the proud mistress of nations, now trembles under the weight of nine successive plagues that have demonstrated the powerlessness of her gods and the supremacy of the Lord God of Israel. The magicians of Pharaoh stand silently defeated, their enchantments proven futile against the mighty hand of the Almighty. Yet the hardened heart of Egypt's king remains unmoved, necessitating one final, terrible visitation that will break the chains of bondage and birth a nation through the crucible of God's judgment.

It is within this atmosphere of mounting dread and desperate hope that the Lord speaks to Moses and Aaron, instituting what would become the most sacred ordinance in Israel's calendar. **The doctrine of the Lamb of God, which began with Abel's acceptable sacrifice and deepened through Abraham's willingness to offer Isaac, now advances to its most comprehensive Old Testament revelation.** The Passover stands as a memorial of past deliverance, and as the foundational revelation of God's redemptive plan, a plan that would find its fulfillment in the sacrifice of the Lamb of God who takes away the sin of the world.

A LAMB FOR EVERY HOUSE

The Lord's instruction to Moses and Aaron carries the weight of eternal purpose: "*Speak ye unto all the congregation of Israel, saying, In the tenth day of this month they shall take to them every man a lamb, according to the house of their fathers, a lamb for an house*" (**Exodus 12:3**).

This command establishes the fundamental principle that redemption is intensely personal and particular. No household could be spared the necessity of the sacrifice; no family could rely upon the obedience of their neighbors.

The lamb selected for this purpose was to meet specific, God-ordained requirements. "*Your lamb shall be without blemish, a male of the first year:*

ye shall take it out from the sheep, or from the goats" (**Exodus 12:5**). The requirement of perfection—"*without blemish"*—**establishes the principle** that God accepts nothing less than absolute purity in His sacrificial offerings. This lamb must be a male in the prime of life, neither too young to have developed strength nor too old to have lost its vigor. The specification of "*the first year"* indicates the sacrifice must be made in the creature's prime, before any defect or weakness could develop.

For four days, from the tenth to the fourteenth of the month, each household was to observe their chosen lamb, ensuring its perfection and growing familiar with its character. This period of examination prefigures the days during which Christ, our Passover Lamb, was scrutinized by His enemies and found without fault. Pilate himself declared, "*I find no fault in this man,"* (**Luke 23:4**) yet proceeded with the crucifixion that God's redemptive plan demanded.

BLOOD UPON THE DOORPOSTS

"And ye shall keep it up until the fourteenth day of the same month: and the whole assembly of the congregation of Israel shall kill it in the evening" (**Exodus 12:6**). The timing is precise and purposeful. As the sun sets and darkness falls, the entire congregation participates simultaneously in this act of sacrifice. No lamb is to be spared; no household excused from this solemn requirement.

The application of the blood follows specific God-given instruction: *"And they shall take of the blood, and strike it on the two side posts and on the upper door post of the houses, wherein they shall eat it"* (**Exodus 12:7**). The blood is not sprinkled carelessly but applied deliberately to form a refuge-like sheltering pattern across the entrance to each dwelling. This mark serves as more than identification; it constitutes a declaration of faith in God's promise and trust in His provision for protection.

The significance of the doorposts cannot be overstated. The doorway represents the boundary between the public sphere and the private sanctuary of the home. By commanding the blood to be placed upon this threshold, God establishes the principle that redemption creates a separation between the redeemed and the unredeemed, between those under God's protection and those exposed to wrath.

EATEN IN HASTE WITH BITTER REMEMBRANCE

The consumption of the sacrifice follows specific ceremonial requirements that reveal typological significance. "*And they shall eat the flesh in that night, roast with fire, and unleavened bread; and with bitter herbs they shall eat it*" (**Exodus 12:8**). Each element of this meal speaks to essential aspects of redemption and the believer's relationship to the sacrifice.

The lamb must be "*roast with fire*"—not eaten raw nor boiled in water, but thoroughly prepared by the intense heat of flame. "*Eat not of it raw, nor sodden at all with water, but roast with fire; his head with his legs, and with the purtenance thereof*" (**Exodus 12:9**). This method of preparation signifies the completeness of the sacrifice and the intensity of judgment that the substitute must bear. Fire, throughout scripture, often represents God's consuming judgment: "*For the LORD thy God is a consuming fire*" (**Deuteronomy 4:24**). The lamb, roasted by fire, prefigures Christ enduring the full heat of the Father's wrath on behalf of sinners.

The bitter herbs serve as a constant reminder of the bitterness of bondage. As each Israelite tasted these herbs, they would remember cruel Egyptian enslavers making life bitter with harsh labor in brick and mortar: "*And they made their lives bitter with hard bondage*" (**Exodus 1:14**). Yet these bitter herbs also point forward to the bitter cup that Christ would drink for our redemption—the cup of wrath He consumed to its dregs: "*Father, if thou be willing, remove this cup from me... nevertheless not my will, but thine, be done*" (**Luke 22:42**).

The unleavened bread speaks of purity and the urgency of deliverance. Leaven, representing corruption and sin, was entirely excluded from this meal: "*Purge out therefore the old leaven... that ye may be a new lump*" (**1 Corinthians 5:7−8**). The bread of haste reminds us that redemption, once provided, demands immediate response and complete commitment.

The entire meal is consumed "*with your loins girded, your shoes on your feet, and your staff in your hand; and ye shall eat it in haste: it is the LORD's passover*" (**Exodus 12:11**). This is no leisurely feast but a meal eaten in readiness for immediate departure. The redeemed people of God must be prepared to leave the land of bondage at a moment's notice when their deliverance comes.

DEATH'S COSTLY VISIT

The climactic moment of this all-too-real drama arrives with the Lord's solemn declaration: "*For I will pass through the land of Egypt this night, and will smite all the firstborn in the land of Egypt... I am the LORD*" (**Exodus 12:12**). This judgment is comprehensive and inescapable. Every house in Egypt—whether belonging to Pharaoh's palace or the humblest Israelite dwelling—will experience the touch of death unless protected by the blood of the lamb.

The universality of this judgment demonstrates the universal nature of sin and its consequences. Rich and poor, mighty and weak, Egyptian and foreigner—all stand equally condemned before God's righteous justice. Only those who have applied the blood **according to God's instruction** will be spared from the destroyer's hand.

"And the blood shall be to you for a token upon the houses... when I see the blood, I will pass over you..." (**Exodus 12:13**). The promise is absolute: where God sees the blood, judgment passes over. The safety of the household depends not upon the moral character of its inhabitants, but upon the presence of the substitutionary sacrifice applied in exact obedience. The blood of **a** lamb was their hope then; the blood of **the** Lamb is our only hope now..

Thus the Passover continues the pattern of redemption established at Abel's altar (**Genesis 4:4**) and tested on Mount Moriah (**Hebrews 11:19**). Just as Abel obeyed God's prescribed offering and Abraham obeyed even unto the point of sacrifice, here the Israelites obey God's command to apply the lamb's blood—and in that obedience they find deliverance. This theme of faith manifest in obedient action undergirds the entire narrative of salvation, from the first blood shed in Eden to the Lamb of God who secures eternal life for all who trust and obey Him.

PROTECTION BY BLOOD

"For the LORD will pass through to smite the Egyptians; and when he seeth the blood upon the lintel, and on the two side posts, the LORD will pass over the door, and will not suffer the destroyer to come in unto your houses to

smite you" (**Exodus 12:23**). The repetition emphasizes the certainty of God's protection where the blood is found. This is not mercy extended to the deserving, but grace provided to those who trust in God's appointed means of salvation.

The contrast could not be more stark. In houses marked by blood, there is safety, protection, and life. In houses without the blood, there is judgment, death, and mourning. The distinction lies, again, not in the moral character of the inhabitants but in their faith in God's promise of protection which inspired their obedience to His clear commands. It is essential to remember that works follow faith, thereby ensuring faith is not dead (**James 2:17**). But, when works attempt to get ahead of faith, this inordinate approach will be rejected and the judgment one falsely hopes to escape will be delivered.

As midnight approaches and the destroyer begins his terrible work, the sounds of Egyptian mourning fill the night air. *"And there was a great cry in Egypt; for there was not a house where there was not one dead"* (**Exodus 12:30**). Yet within the blood-marked homes of Israel, there is peace, safety, and anticipation of the deliverance to come. As Israel passed from death to life by a lamb's blood, so believers pass from death to life by the Lamb of God's blood. Herein lies the solemn truth of redemption: **faith is not a trivial matter**, but the very hinge upon which the door of deliverance swings open or shut.

THE MEMORIAL

The Lord's command extends beyond this single night to establish a perpetual memorial: *"And this day shall be unto you for a memorial; and ye shall keep it a feast to the LORD throughout your generations; ye shall keep it a feast by an ordinance for ever"* (**Exodus 12:14**). The Passover becomes more than a historical event; it transforms into a teaching institution designed to transmit the knowledge of God's redemptive work to every succeeding generation.

This educational purpose becomes explicit in God's instruction for future observances: *"And it shall come to pass, when your children shall say unto you, What mean ye by this service? That ye shall say, It is the sacrifice of the LORD's passover, who passed over the houses of the children of Israel in Egypt"* (**Exodus 12:26-27**). Each family becomes a classroom where parents recount how the blood on their doorposts spared them from death, ensuring that the doctrine of redemption through substitutionary sacrifice passes from father to son throughout all generations.

The feast of unleavened bread, lasting seven days, serves as an extended reminder of the urgency and purity required in God's service. *"Seven days shall ye eat unleavened bread; even the first day ye shall put away leaven out of your houses: for whosoever eateth leavened bread from the first day until the seventh day, that soul shall be cut off from Israel"* (**Exodus 12:15**). The complete removal of leaven symbolizes the thoroughness with which sin must be purged from the life of the redeemed—not a hasty remembrance of Egypt's exit, but a lasting emblem of purity that foreshadows the believer's call to *"purge out therefore the old leaven... that ye may be a new lump"* (**1 Corinthians 5:7**).

Thus the Passover memorial builds upon the progressive revelation established through Abel's blood sacrifice and Abraham's substitutionary offering, creating a comprehensive pattern of atonement, provision, and generational teaching that would culminate in Christ's own words: *"This do in remembrance of me"* (**Luke 22:19**). The same God who commanded Israel to remember their deliverance through the lamb's blood would establish the Lord's Supper as the memorial of our deliverance through the Lamb of God.

CHRIST OUR PASSOVER

The apostolic writings leave no uncertainty regarding the ultimate significance of the Passover lamb. "*For even Christ our passover is sacrificed for us: Therefore let us keep the feast, not with old leaven, neither with the leaven of malice and wickedness; but with the unleavened bread of sincerity and truth*" (**1 Corinthians 5:7-8**). Paul declares explicitly that Christ is the true Passover Lamb, the reality of which every Paschal sacrifice was but a shadow.

John the Baptist's declaration rings with prophetic clarity: "*Behold the Lamb of God, which taketh away the sin of the world*" (**John 1:29**). Just as the Passover lamb was selected, examined, slain, and consumed, so Christ was chosen before the foundation of the world, scrutinized by His enemies, crucified for our redemption, and spiritually received by faith.

The precision of prophetic fulfillment astounds the careful student. Christ entered Jerusalem on the tenth day of Nisan (**Matthew 21:1-6, John 12:12-13**), exactly when the Passover lambs were selected. Then He was examined by Pharisees, Sadducees, Herodians, and Romans, yet no fault was found in Him. On the fourteenth day, at the same hour the Passover lambs were being slain, He gave up the ghost on Calvary's cross (**John 19:30**).

Even the details of His crucifixion fulfilled the Passover typology with stunning accuracy. "*But when they came to Jesus, and saw that he was dead already, they brake not his legs*" (**John 19:33**), fulfilling the requirement that not a bone of the Passover lamb should be broken. His blood, shed for the remission of sins, provides eternal protection from the wrath of God for all who trust in His sacrifice. Thus, having been redeemed by Christ our Passover Lamb, we are called to live with sincerity and truth—casting off malice and wickedness—and to walk daily in the power of His atoning blood.

THE CONTRAST OF GRACE AND JUDGMENT

The Passover vividly illustrates that God's justice and mercy intersect at the sacrifice of the Lamb—every sinner stands condemned by justice unless covered by Christ's atoning blood. The institution of the Passover lays bare God's twofold character: **His unblemished justice demands the death of the guilty**, and **His boundless mercy supplies a Substitute**. Each Israelite household confronted a decisive choice—apply the blood of the lamb and live, or refuse it and perish under God's righteous wrath. There was no neutral ground, no merit of human effort, no alternative sacrifice.

This inexorable division remains unchanged in the New Covenant. "*Being justified by his blood, we shall be saved from wrath through him*" (**Romans 5:9**). As then the blood on the doorposts signified acceptance of God's provision, so now faith in Christ's blood secures complete immunity from God's judgment. "*Whom God hath set forth to be a propitiation through faith in his blood, to declare his righteousness*" (**Romans 3:25–26**). No human striving or ritual can suffice; Christ's single offering "*hath perfected for ever them that are sanctified*" (**Hebrews 10:14**).

The night of Passover declares that God's love does not annul justice but satisfies it. The lamb died so that Israel's firstborn might live; Christ died that sinners might be redeemed. In both, wrath falls—but upon the Substitute, never upon those who rest in God's gracious provision.

THE FOUNDATION FOR FUTURE REVELATION

The Passover is far more than a historical deliverance; it serves as godly paradigm for salvation, introducing the core principles that define God's redemptive work. In **Exodus 12**—the necessity of a perfect sacrifice, the requirement of blood for atonement, the personal application of redemption, the memorial character of salvation, and the protection from God's wrath—find their ultimate expression in the work of Christ.

Every Old Testament sacrifice, every ceremonial washing, every feast and fast points back to the Passover and forward to Calvary. The scarlet thread of redemption that runs through scripture has its visible beginning in the blood applied to the doorposts of Israel and finds its glorious culmination in the blood of the Lamb of God shed for the sins of the world.

The Passover serves as God's elementary school in the doctrine of substitutionary atonement. Through this vivid, historical demonstration, He teaches His people that sin requires death, that the innocent may die for the guilty, that blood must be shed for forgiveness, and that those who trust in His provision will be spared from judgment. These lessons, learned in the crucible of Israel's bondage and deliverance, prepare God's people to understand and receive the greater salvation that would come through the sacrifice of His only begotten Son.

As we contemplate this sacred narrative, we are reminded that the God who delivered Israel from Egyptian bondage continues to deliver sinners from the bondage of sin through the blood of the Lamb. The same certainty that protected the Israelites—*"when I see the blood, I will pass over you"*—continues to shield all who trust in Christ's sacrifice. Where His blood is applied by faith, judgment passes over, and the redeemed soul finds safety, peace, and eternal life in the shelter of the Almighty.

CHAPTER FOUR

THE LAMB FROM LEVITICUS TO CHRIST

The Book of Leviticus will elaborate God's comprehensive sacrificial system, revealing how the burnt offering, peace offering, sin offering, and trespass offering each prefigured distinct aspects of Christ's multifaceted redemptive work.

THE BLUEPRINT

T O THE MODERN MIND, the book of **Leviticus** often appears as a dusty and bewildering relic, a collection of arcane rituals and prohibitions long since rendered obsolete. Yet to dismiss it as such is to fundamentally misdiagnose the human condition it so unflinchingly addresses. For within its seemingly impenetrable pages lies the blueprint for a bridge, spanning the terrifying chasm between a holy God and a sinful humanity. Having been brought out of bondage, Israel was confronted not with liberty alone, but with a far more difficult question: **how does an imperfect people draw near to the consuming fire of perfection without being utterly destroyed?** Leviticus is God's severe and merciful answer, a *"shadow of good things to come"* (**Hebrews**

10:1) that furnishes the pattern and promise of the true and living Sacrifice.

The book's statutes are built upon two immense pillars, which bear the entire weight of redemptive history. **The first** is the staggering, unalterable **holiness of God**, a truth that rings like a solemn bell through every ordinance: *"for I the LORD your God am holy"* (**Leviticus 19:2**). **The second** is the soul's only means of **access through sacrifice**, a principle sealed in blood: *"for the life of the flesh is in the blood...it is the blood that maketh an atonement for the soul"* (**Leviticus 17:11**). Thus, what might seem at first to be a trivial ceremony reveals itself upon closer inspection to be a detailed anatomy of the gospel, **rendered in the types and shadows of the Old Testament**. Every ritual, from the inspection of a blemish to the sprinkling of blood, magnifies these twin truths, guiding the worshiper's soul from the endless repetition of animal sacrifice toward the final, *"once-for-all"* oblation of the Lamb of God.

A PROGRESSIVE REVELATION: THE SCARLET THREAD

The revelation of the Lamb of God unfolds progressively through scripture, with each stage unveiling a new aspect of His redemptive work. **Leviticus** systematizes these lessons, establishing enduring types that converge on Jesus Christ with increasing precision.

Genesis 4: The acceptable approach to God must be by blood (**Genesis 4:4**).

Genesis 22: The Lamb is God's provision—"God will provide himself a lamb" (**Genesis 22:8**).

Exodus 12: The Passover Lamb is the believer's protection from judgment (**Exodus 12:5**).

Leviticus 16–22: The Lamb's perfection is demanded for sin to be removed (**Leviticus 22:21**).

Isaiah 53: The Lamb is the silent, substitutionary sufferer (**Isaiah 53:7**).

John 1: The Lamb is publicly identified as the Son of God (**John 1:29**).

1 Peter 1: The Lamb's precious blood is the price of our redemption (**1 Peter 1:19**).

Revelation 5: The slain Lamb is the enthroned Redeemer, worthy of all worship (**Revelation 5:6**).

Revelation 22: The Lamb's throne is the eternal home and source of light for the saints (**Revelation 22:1**).

LEVITICUS 22:17-25—THE PERFECTION MANDATE

The entire sacrificial system is erected upon a single, unyielding foundation: **the principle of unblemished perfection**. God's standard is not a vague aspiration but a non-negotiable mandate. Any offering brought before the LORD, whether from an Israelite or a stranger in Israel, must be *"a male without blemish"* (**Leviticus 22:19**). This was not a matter of aesthetic preference but of profound significance. By demanding the *"best"*—the flawless, the whole, the most valuable—God was teaching a lesson etched into the very fabric of the economy of grace: that sin, being a corruption, can only be atoned for by incorruption. The worshiper could not bring his cast-offs, the lame animal he could not sell at market, or the blind one that was a drain on his resources. To do so would be to offer a blemished solution to the problem of blemish, a flawed answer to the question of sin.

The prohibitions are exhaustive and visceral: *"Blind, or broken, or maimed, or having a wen, or scurvy, or scabbed, ye shall not offer these unto the LORD"* (**Leviticus 22:22**). Each physical defect served as a tangible, vivid sermon on the nature of spiritual imperfection. Just as these visible flaws rendered an animal unfit for the altar, so too does any moral or spiritual flaw render a person unfit for the presence of a holy God. This relentless focus on external perfection was designed to cultivate an internal awareness of sin's disfiguring nature and the absolute perfection required to stand before a God who is Himself without spot or wrinkle. The requirement was absolute because the One to whom the offering was made is absolute.

This mandate of perfection is not only a procedural rule; it is a rich text in itself, bearing three profound doctrinal implications that form the bedrock of the gospel.

First, it reveals the catastrophic nature of sin. In our modern therapeutic culture, sin is often minimized to a simple mistake, a poor choice, or a psychological failing. The Levitical standard corrects this shallow diagnosis with severe clarity. If the *symbol* of atonement—an animal—had to be physically flawless, it forces the worshiper to confront the destructive nature of the spiritual reality it addresses. Sin is not a slight imperfection but a deep corruption, a malignant blemish on the soul that constitutes a catastrophic offense against the perfect holiness of God. The high cost of the sacrifice, requiring the best of one's flock, taught Israel that rectifying this offense was no small matter; it demanded the forfeiture of something precious, driving home the gravity of the debt that was owed.

Second, it relentlessly foreshadows the unique perfection of Christ. The demand for an unblemished lamb, repeated across generations, was a prophecy spoken not in words but in ritual. It cultivated a deep, collective anticipation for a final, perfect sacrifice that could truly suffice. This expectation finds its ultimate fulfillment in Jesus Christ, the *"lamb without blemish and without spot"* (**1 Peter 1:19**). When Pontius Pilate, the pragmatic Roman governor, examined Jesus and declared with unwitting finality, *"I find no fault in this man"* (**Luke 23:4**), he was unknowingly acting on behalf of the Levitical system, inspecting the final sacrifice for all humanity and declaring it fit for the altar. Christ's perfection was not only the absence of external defect; it was a complete and comprehensive holiness that permeated His nature, character, thoughts, words, and deeds, making Him the only one in human history truly qualified to be the substitute.

Finally, it reveals the profound paradox of God's justice and grace. The unyielding demand for a perfect sacrifice establishes a standard that man, in its fallen and blemished state, could never hope to meet. This requirement was not designed to be a ladder for man to climb to God, but rather a mirror to show him how far he had fallen and the utter futility of his own efforts. Yet, in this very mandate lies the embryo of the gospel: **the same God who required the flawless offering would, in the fullness of time, *become* the flawless offering.** This principle demonstrates that salvation is not a cooperative effort but a radical act of initiative, wherein God Himself provides the very thing His own holiness demands, meeting His righteous standard on our behalf.

THE FIVE CORE OFFERINGS AND THE LAMB

The Levitical system prescribed five distinct offerings, each revealing a different aspect of Christ's redemptive work.

The Burnt Offering (Leviticus 1): This offering required the complete consumption of *"a male without blemish"* upon the altar, representing total consecration to God. It typified Christ's absolute surrender to the Father's will as a *"sweetsmelling savour"* (**Ephesians 5:2**). The laying on of hands (**Leviticus 1:4**) prefigured the transfer of sin to the perfect Substitute.

The Meat/Grain Offering (Leviticus 2): Composed of fine flour, oil, and frankincense, this bloodless offering represented the perfect, sinless humanity of Christ. It was an act of thanksgiving that foreshadowed Christ as the *"bread of life"* (**John 6:35**), with the fine flour signifying His pure life, the oil representing the Spirit's anointing, and the frankincense symbolizing His fragrant obedience.

The Peace Offering (Leviticus 3): This offering established communion between God and the worshiper through a shared meal. Partially burned on the altar and partially consumed by the priest and offerer, it prefigured Christ as *"our peace"* (**Ephesians 2:14**), who reconciled man to God and established fellowship through His blood.

The Sin Offering (Leviticus 4): Providing atonement for specific transgressions, this offering of a *"female without blemish"* foreshadowed Christ, who *"knew no sin"* but was *"made sin for us"* (**2 Corinthians 5:21**). The application of blood to the altar's horns demonstrated that specific sins required a specific, atoning sacrifice.

The Trespass Offering (Leviticus 5-6): This offering emphasized restitution for wrongs against God and man, requiring *"a ram without blemish."* It typified Christ, who not only bore our guilt but made full payment for our sin-debt, *"blotting out the handwriting of ordinances that was against us...nailing it to his cross"* (**Colossians 2:14**).

LEVITICUS 16—THE DAY OF ATONEMENT

The Day of Atonement arose after the tragic death of Aaron's sons, who offered *"strange fire"* before God (**Leviticus 10:1**), serving as a solemn reminder of His holiness. On this one day of the year, the high priest entered the Holy of Holies. His preparation involved washing and donning simple linen garments, symbolizing the humility required to represent a sinful people and prefiguring Christ's incarnation, when He *"took upon him the form of a servant"* (**Philippians 2:7**).

Yet, in the very heart of this solemn ceremony lies a detail of shattering significance, one that exposes the fatal flaw in the entire Levitical system. Before the high priest could even begin to intercede for the nation, he first had to offer a bullock as a sin offering *for himself*. This was the man who stood at the apex of Israel's spiritual life, the one chosen to enter the very presence of God. He was supposed to be, by all human standards, the best and most consecrated among them. And yet, he was a man compassed with infirmity, a sinner in need of atonement just like the people he represented.

This requirement serves as a stark and humbling reminder that no human system, no matter how godly the intent, can ultimately bridge the chasm between God and man. If the holiest man in the nation was himself tainted by sin and required a sacrifice before he could even begin his work, what hope could there be for the rest of humanity? The law, in this moment, becomes a profound tutor, demonstrating not its sufficiency, but its glorious insufficiency. It proves that the problem of sin is too deep to be solved by a sinful mediator. This act was a silent, annual prophecy, pointing beyond itself to the desperate need for a different kind of High Priest—one who was not only *"holy, harmless, undefiled, separate from sinners,"* but who would need no sacrifice for His own sins, because He had none. It highlights the inescapable truth that we are not only in need of a better representative; we are in need of a perfect Savior.

FOR THE PEOPLE, TWO GOATS WERE PRESENTED.

The Goat for the LORD: This goat was sacrificed as a sin offering, and its blood was carried into the Holy of Holies and sprinkled on the mercy seat. This act demonstrated that God's justice must be satisfied through a substitutionary death, prefiguring the blood of Christ that permanently satisfies God's wrath for all who believe.

The Scapegoat: The high priest laid his hands on the head of the live goat, confessing over it all the iniquities of Israel. The goat was then sent away *"unto a land not inhabited"* (**Leviticus 16:22**), bearing their sins away. This illustrated the complete removal of sin, which Christ accomplished when He bore our sins away, removing them *"as far as the east is from the west"* (**Psalm 103:12**).

The day concluded with a Sabbath of rest, symbolizing the peace that follows atonement—a peace eternally secured by Christ's perfect work.

FROM SHADOW TO SUBSTANCE: THE SUPERIORITY OF CHRIST'S PRIESTHOOD IN HEBREWS

The book of **Hebrews** serves as God's own commentary on **Leviticus**, drawing a sharp and glorious contrast between the perpetual, unfinished work of the Levitical priesthood and the perfect, finished work of Jesus Christ. The writer highlights several points of superiority that demonstrate the finality of Christ's sacrifice.

A Standing Priest vs. a Seated Savior: The Levitical priest's work was never done; therefore, he *always stood*, ministering daily and offering sacrifices that could never truly take away sin. In stark contrast, Christ, having completed the work of redemption, *"sat down on the right hand of God,"* signifying His work was finished completely and accepted forever **(Hebrews 10:11-12)**.

Repeated Sacrifices vs. a Once-for-All Offering: The Aaronic priesthood was characterized by endless repetition—daily, monthly, and yearly offerings that served as a constant reminder that sin was never truly dealt with. But Christ, *"after he had offered **one sacrifice for sins for ever**,"* made all other sacrifices obsolete **(Hebrews 10:12)**. His single offering was infinitely sufficient.

The Blood of Animals vs. the Blood of God's Son: The Old Covenant operated on a foundational, yet limited, truth: animal blood could cover sin ceremonially, but it could never remove it. The Holy Spirit taught this explicitly, for *"it is not possible that the blood of bulls and of goats should take away sins"* **(Hebrews 10:4)**. Christ, however, entered the heavenly sanctuary not with the blood of animals, but with His own **blood**, thereby obtaining eternal redemption **(Hebrews 9:12)**.

Striving Worshipers vs. a Perfected People: The Levitical sacrifices could never make those who drew near *"perfect"* in their standing before God. The system was designed to expose sin, not grant ultimate peace. Yet, by Christ's singular work, the believer's standing before God is eternally secured, for *"by one offering he hath **perfected for ever** them that are sanctified"* (**Hebrews 10:14**).

A Frail Priest vs. a Flawless High Priest: The high priests of old were men *"compassed with infirmity,"* who had to offer sacrifices for their own sins first. But we have *"such an high priest, who is **holy, harmless, undefiled, separate from sinners,** and made higher than the heavens"* (**Hebrews 7:26**). His personal perfection guarantees the eternal security of ours.

DISPELLING ENDURING MISCONCEPTIONS

The sacrificial system of **Leviticus,** seen through the clarifying lens of the New Testament, is a profound teacher. However, its distance from our modern world often gives rise to several persistent misunderstandings about God, salvation, and the Christian life. To fully grasp the doctrine of the Lamb, we must clear away these common errors.

A foundational error is the belief that Old Testament saints were saved by meticulously keeping the Law. This view demotes the Law to a checklist of religious duties, which, if performed correctly, would earn a person favor with God. The Bible, however, presents the Law in a different light. It was never intended as a means of salvation; rather, it functioned as a mirror, revealing the holy character of God and, in contrast, the profound depth of human sinfulness. Far from being a ladder to God, the Law was a diagnosis of man's fallen condition, demonstrating his inability to save himself and thus pointing him relentlessly toward his need for a blood sacrifice, for *"without shedding of blood is no remission"* (**Hebrews 9:22**).

This leads to a second misconception: **that the Levitical sacrifices themselves were sufficient to permanently take away sin.** If the Law showed the disease, the sacrifices were seen as the cure. But the writer of **Hebrews** is explicit: *"it is not possible that the blood of bulls and of goats should take away sins"* (**Hebrews 10:4**). These offerings provided a temporary, ceremonial cleansing that allowed the life of the nation to continue in God's presence, in the promised land, but they could never remove the ultimate guilt or cleanse the conscience. They were a perpetual reminder of sin's debt, not a final payment. The very fact that they had to be repeated year after year was a testament to their glorious insufficiency, a shadow that proved the necessity of a coming substance.

Another misunderstanding can arise from the haunting figure of the scapegoat on the Day of Atonement. Its dramatic journey into the wilderness has led to various interpretations, but its core purpose is one of beautiful simplicity. The scapegoat being sent *"unto a land not inhabited"* was a powerful, tangible illustration of sin's **complete removal** from God's sight. The first goat satisfied God's justice through its death; the second goat demonstrated the consequence of that satisfaction for the believer—the total banishment of confessed sin. It powerfully declared the comprehensive nature of a true atonement.

Finally, the Levitical demand for perfection often creates confusion for New Testament believers, who can feel crushed by a standard they know they cannot meet. This gives rise to the idea that perfection is an unrealistic and ungracious burden. The crucial distinction that must be made, however, is between our *standing* and our *state*. In Christ, because of His perfect, finished work, the believer is granted an immediate and eternal **judicial perfection**. Before God's throne of justice, we are seen as righteous, "perfected for ever" by Christ's one offering (**Hebrews 10:14**). This is our unshakeable standing. In our daily lives, however, we are called to a life of **practical holiness**, not to earn our salvation, but as a response to it. We pursue holiness not to achieve a perfect standing, but because we have already been given one, now empowered by the Holy Spirit to live in a way that reflects the new identity we have received in Christ (**1 Peter 1:15-16**).

GLORYING IN THE BETTER SACRIFICE

Leviticus preaches Christ with every ceremony and every drop of blood. Its insistence on flawless lambs and its solemn Day of Atonement all converge at Calvary, where the sinless Son offered Himself "*once for all*" (**Hebrews 7:27**). The shadows have served their purpose; the substance has come. The promise has been kept; the Lamb has been provided.

Therefore, we can approach the throne of grace with boldness, knowing our great High Priest has entered the holy place on our behalf (**Hebrews 4:16**). Until the day the Lamb on the throne leads us to "*living fountains of waters*" (**Revelation 7:17**), may our lives testify that our sins are removed, fellowship is secured, and the perfect Lamb of God is worthy of unceasing praise. "*Worthy is the Lamb that was slain to receive power, and riches, and wisdom, and strength, and honour, and glory, and blessing*" (**Revelation 5:12**). To Him be glory both now and forever. Amen.

CHAPTER FIVE

THE LAMB, THE PERSON

Isaiah 53 will provide scripture's most detailed prophetic portrait of the suffering Servant, revealing both the Lamb's voluntary anguish and His victorious accomplishment in bearing the sins of many.

THE OLD TESTAMENT PORTRAIT

ISAIAH **53**, SCRIPTURE'S MAJESTIC Old Testament portrait of **Jesus Christ as the Lamb of God**. Seven centuries before the Word became flesh and dwelt among us, the Holy Ghost sketched through the prophet's pen a vivid depiction of the life, suffering, death, and triumph of Him whom John the Baptist would identify beside Jordan's waters as *"the Lamb of God, which taketh away the sin of the world"* (**John 1:29**). This chapter provides the Bible's clearest Old Testament revelation of substitutionary atonement, unveiling the foundation upon which rests the entire dispensation of grace. Herein we encounter the mystery of godliness: **God was manifest in the flesh as the Lamb who was slain for the sins of the world (1 Timothy 3:16).**

THE FORBIDDEN CHAPTER IN JEWISH TRADITION

Isaiah 53 has earned the sobriquet *"The Forbidden Chapter"* in Jewish tradition, a testament to its overwhelming messianic clarity. The ancient rabbis regularly read this passage in synagogues until its implications became too evident to ignore. As the 17th-century Jewish historian Raphael Levi documented, the chapter eventually *"caused arguments and great confusion"* among the congregants due to its unmistakable portrayal of a suffering Messiah. The rabbis' solution proved as telling as it was tragic: **remove the prophecy from the Haftarah readings altogether**.

Today, when reading through **Isaiah** in many synagogues, the liturgy typically advances from **chapter 52** directly to **chapter 54**, deliberately omitting this profound messianic text. This systematic suppression reveals the chapter's power and clarity. Ancient rabbis understood **Isaiah 53** to speak of the Messiah. The Babylonian Talmud explicitly declared, *"The Messiah, what is his name? The Rabbis say, The Leper Scholar, as it is said, 'surely he has borne our griefs and carried our sorrows: yet we did esteem him a leper, smitten of God and afflicted"*. The Targum Jonathan rendered **Isaiah 52:13** as *"Behold my servant Messiah shall prosper"*.

Yet when Jesus of Nazareth appeared, fulfilling these prophecies with startling precision, the passage became inconvenient truth. The classical Jewish position on the suffering Messiah found its expression in the words of medieval Jewish commentators, who declared that the Messiah willingly accepts suffering upon himself: *"As he himself desires to carry them... And we thought of him as he would not take them upon himself, only he who is afflicted and smitten by God. But when the time will come for him to reveal himself in all his glory, then all will see and understand how great is the strength of the one who suffers for his generation"*. This ancient recognition of a suffering Messiah makes modern Jewish rejection of Jesus all the more poignant.

THE FOUR SERVANT SONGS OF ISAIAH

Isaiah 53 represents the culminating fourth song in a series of prophetic portraits known as the Servant Songs. These four passages (**Isaiah 42:1-4; 49:1-6; 50:4-9;** and **52:13-53:12**) progressively reveal the character, mission, and ultimate triumph of God's chosen Servant. The development across these songs moves from the Servant's gentle calling and weighty mission (**Isaiah 42**) through His role as Israel's light and the nations' salvation (**Isaiah 49**), to His obedient suffering and determination (**Isaiah 50**), culminating in the detailed portrait of His atoning death and exaltation (**Isaiah 52:13-53:12**).

The fourth Servant Song stands apart in its graphic depiction of vicarious suffering. While the earlier songs hint at the Servant's commission and character, **Isaiah 53** unveils the mechanism by which He accomplishes redemption. The chapter presents suffering, not as martyrdom, but as **substitutionary atonement**—the innocent bearing the punishment of the guilty by God's design. This doctrinal precision places **Isaiah 53** at the heart of biblical soteriology.

THE ARM OF THE LORD (ISAIAH 53:1-3)

THE MYSTERIOUS REPORT

"Who hath believed our report? and to whom is the arm of the LORD revealed?" (**Isaiah 53:1**)

Isaiah begins his portrait with rhetorical questions that anticipate the widespread unbelief that would greet the Messiah. The prophet foresees that God's revelation of ultimate power through a suffering Servant would contradict human expectations of conquest and glory. The Apostle Paul later quoted this verse to explain Israel's current judicial blindness during the times of the Gentiles: *"But they have not all obeyed the gospel. For Esaias saith, Lord, who hath believed our report?"* (**Romans 10:16**).

The phrase *"arm of the LORD"* represents God's strength, power, and might. In the context of the suffering Messiah, this expression reveals the profound mystery of the gospel: God's ultimate power manifested through apparent weakness. The strength of Jehovah would be *"revealed"* not through military conquest but through sacrificial love. This paradox forms the doctrinal backdrop for the entire chapter—great power displayed in suffering, victory achieved through apparent defeat.

THE TENDER PLANT FROM DRY GROUND

"For he shall grow up before him as a tender plant, and as a root out of a dry ground: he hath no form nor comeliness; and when we shall see him, there is no beauty that we should desire him." (**Isaiah 53:2**)

The Messiah's humble origins find expression through agricultural imagery that emphasizes vulnerability rather than strength. A *"tender plant"* suggests fragility and insignificance—the very opposite of earthly majesty. The *"dry ground"* potentially refers to the spiritual barrenness of Israel at the time of Christ's first advent. Jesus indeed grew up in Galilee, a region dismissed as incapable of producing anything significant (**John 1:46**).

The declaration *"he hath no form nor comeliness"* indicates that the Messiah would possess no extraordinary physical attractiveness or outward majesty that would draw natural human admiration. This challenges man's tendency to judge by appearances and reveals that God's values transcend human standards of beauty and power. Jesus' true beauty lay not in physical form but in spiritual character, words, and works. His appearance was that of an ordinary man in His day, enabling Him to move among men without the distraction of superficial glamour.

This ordinary appearance, however, was but the prelude to a far deeper reality. The same prophet who described His lack of outward comeliness also foresaw the violent disfigurement that would render Him unrecognizable. In a prophecy of shocking intensity, Isaiah declared, *"his visage was so marred more than any man, and his form more than the sons of men"* (**Isaiah 52:14**). The *"tender plant"* would be so brutally handled that He would lose the very appearance of a man. This was the horrific cost of substitution. The psalmist, seeing the scourging with prophetic eyes, lamented, *"The plowers plowed upon my back: they made long their furrows"* (**Psalm 129:3**). The back of the sinless Son of God would be plowed like a field, each furrow in His flesh a testament to the sins He bore. This terrible transformation from an ordinary man into a spectacle of suffering was the payment for transgression. He who possessed no superficial beauty to attract sinners was willingly marred beyond recognition to redeem them.

THE MAN OF SORROWS

"He is despised and rejected of men; a man of sorrows, and acquainted with grief: and we hid as it were our faces from him; he was despised, and we esteemed him not." (**Isaiah 53:3**)

In the solemn gallery of messianic prophecy, no portrait is more poignant or penetrating than that of the Man of Sorrows. **Isaiah**, guided by the Holy Ghost, dips his pen in the ink of deep grief to sketch the reception the Lamb of God would receive from a world He came to redeem. The prophet's words are not a cold prediction; they are a lament, a sorrowful insight into the heart of God and the blindness of man.

Here, the Spirit of God unveils the profound and painful paradox of the incarnation. The repetition of the word **"despised"** tolls like a funeral bell, emphasizing the unrelenting and venomous rejection the Messiah would endure. This was not a passive disregard but an active, scornful contempt. He was not simply overlooked; He was loathed. The source of this contempt makes it all the more tragic: it was *"of men,"* the very creatures He had formed and the chosen people He had come to save. Throughout His earthly ministry, Christ was indeed *"rejected of men,"* a rejection that swelled from the whispered doubts in Galilean synagogues to the roaring crowds in Jerusalem demanding His blood. This culminated in His arrest, trial, and crucifixion by the very hands He had come to bless.

The designation *"a man of sorrows, and acquainted with grief"* strikes even deeper, revealing that suffering was not only an event in the Messiah's life but the very atmosphere He breathed. He was not a casual observer of sorrow **but its intimate companion**, personally *"acquainted"* with it in its every form. These were not the common griefs of mankind, but sorrows of a unique and substitutionary nature. He bore *our* griefs and carried *our* sorrows, willingly taking upon Himself the crushing weight of a world's sin and anguish. Every tear He shed was for a world that would not weep for itself; every pang of grief He felt was an echo of the judgment we deserved. His sorrow was the righteous sorrow of a holy God dwelling amongst sinful men, pained by their unbelief and rebellion.

The prophet then turns the lens upon humanity's reaction: *"and we hid as it were our faces from him."* This phrase captures the instinctive, shameful recoil of fallen man from the sight of vicarious suffering. Confronted with the Lamb bearing the penalty for sin, men find the spectacle unbearable. It is a portrait of aversion, a deliberate turning away from the One who turned His face toward Jerusalem to die for them. This was fulfilled with chilling literality as soldiers and scoffers mocked, spat upon, and turned their backs on Jesus throughout His ministry, false arrest, mock trial, and cruel crucifixion. The religious leaders, who should have recognized and welcomed their King, became His most ardent opponents, fulfilling the sorrowful prediction that He would be *"esteemed not"*. Yet, the most piercing fulfillment of this prophecy came when, in the hour of His greatest need, His own disciples *"forsook him, and fled."* In that garden, even those who loved Him hid their faces, unwilling to be associated with the Man of Sorrows and the cross He was determined to bear.

THE SERVANT'S SUBSTITUTIONARY NATURE (ISAIAH 53:4-6)

THE GREAT EXCHANGE

"Surely he hath borne our griefs, and carried our sorrows: yet we did esteem him stricken, smitten of God, and afflicted. But he was wounded for our transgressions, he was bruised for our iniquities: the chastisement of our peace was upon him; and with his stripes we are healed." (**Isaiah 53:4-5**)

In the heart of this prophecy, we find the very essence of the gospel—the Great Exchange. Here, the Spirit of God moves from the world's tragic misjudgment of the Messiah to the eternal transaction that occurred upon the cross. This is not theological abstraction; it is the explanation for the most pivotal event in human history.

The verse begins with a word of emphatic certainty: *"Surely."* This is God's solemn affirmation, correcting humanity's flawed verdict. While men saw a criminal justly punished, God declares the Servant was actively and willingly taking upon Himself that which belonged to others. He *"hath borne our griefs, and carried our sorrows"*. These are not poetic terms; they are words of substitution. He did not simply sympathize with our sorrows; He took them as His own, lifting the crushing weight of our spiritual and emotional anguish and placing it upon His own sinless soul. This was not the act of a martyr suffering for a cause, but the act of an innocent Substitute suffering for the guilty. Yet, in our spiritual blindness, *"we did esteem him stricken, smitten of God, and afflicted"*—we judged Him to be receiving punishment for His own transgressions, when in reality, He was absorbing the very wrath of God that we deserved.

The prophet then unveils the purpose behind this suffering with four declarations of substitutionary atonement, each a facet of the same glorious jewel :

"He was wounded for our transgressions." The word *"wounded"* here speaks of a violent piercing. It was for *our* rebellions, our willful defiance of God's law, that His hands, feet, and side were pierced.

"He was bruised for our iniquities." This refers to the crushing weight of punishment. His body and soul were crushed under the load of *our* sin against God.

"The chastisement of our peace was upon him." The punishment that was necessary to bring about our reconciliation with a holy God fell entirely upon Him. He endured the full measure of wrath so that we might have peace *with* God.

"With his stripes we are healed." The bloody wounds left by the scourging, the "stripes," became the very source of our spiritual healing. His physical agony purchased our spiritual wholeness.

Let the soul who reads these words pause and consider the staggering depth of this exchange. Your rebellion caused His wounding. Your guilt caused His bruising. Your separation from God required His chastisement. Every sin you have ever committed was laid upon Him. This is the heart of the gospel: **the innocent for the guilty, the righteous for the unrighteous, the beloved Son for the rebellious sinner**. This is a truth and a reality to be embraced with a broken and a contrite heart.

UNIVERSAL GUILT, SINGULAR SUBSTITUTE

"All we like sheep have gone astray; we have turned every one to his own way; and the LORD hath laid on him the iniquity of us all." (**Isaiah 53:6**)

This verse presents both the universal human condition and God's singular remedy. The sheep imagery connects to the sacrificial system while emphasizing man's propensity to wander from truth. "*All we like sheep have gone astray*" describes the collective rebellion of mankind against God's righteous standards. "*We have turned every one to his own way"* emphasizes the individual nature of sin—each person choosing their own direction rather than God's way.

This impulse to go *"our own way"* is not a recent development; it is the ancient and tragic inheritance of the fall. In the cool of the day, after their rebellion, Adam and Eve heard the voice of the LORD God walking in the garden. But instead of running to Him in fellowship, *"Adam and his wife hid themselves from the presence of the LORD God amongst the trees of the garden"* (**Genesis 3:8**). Their physical hiding was the outward expression of an inward turning. When God called, *"Where art thou?"* He exposes this propensity for man to go his own way. In that moment, they had chosen their own path, a direction that leads not to communion with God, but to separation from Him. Isaiah's declaration, therefore, is the diagnosis of a spiritual disease that has infected every human heart since Eden. *"His own way"* is any path that turns from the face of God, and we have all, every one, chosen that path of shameful hiding over holy fellowship.

The final clause reveals God's active role in the atonement: *"the LORD hath laid on him the iniquity of us all"*. Our sins were deliberately and purposefully placed upon the Messiah as part of God's eternal redemptive plan. This represents the heart of substitutionary atonement—the innocent voluntarily bearing the punishment deserved by the guilty through godly appointment. This was a violent encounter or meeting, indicating the full weight of man's sin converging upon the sinless Servant.

THE SERVANT'S WILLING SUBMISSION (ISAIAH 53:7-9)

THE LAMB LED TO SLAUGHTER

"He was oppressed, and he was afflicted, yet he opened not his mouth: he is brought as a lamb to the slaughter, and as a sheep before her shearers is dumb, so he openeth not his mouth." (**Isaiah 53:7**)

Here we encounter the explicit comparison of the Suffering Servant to a sacrificial lamb, providing the bridge between the Levitical offerings and the Lamb of God. The Servant's silence receives double emphasis: *"he opened not his mouth"* and *"so he openeth not his mouth"*. This silence was not inability to speak but deliberate submission to God's redemptive will.

The phrase *"as a lamb to the slaughter"* directly connects the Suffering Servant to the sacrificial lambs that pointed forward to the ultimate sacrifice. John the Baptist recognized this connection when he said, *"Behold the Lamb of God, which taketh away the sin of the world"* (**John 1:29**). The lamb imagery encompasses both the Passover lamb that delivered Israel from death and the daily sacrificial lambs that maintained fellowship with God.

Jesus remarkably fulfilled this prophecy during His trials before the Sanhedrin, Herod, and Pilate. Though falsely accused, He remained largely silent, choosing not to defend Himself though He possessed the wisdom to confound His accusers. His silence represented not weakness but strength—the deliberate choice of the Son of God to submit to the Father's plan of redemption.

CUT OFF FROM THE LAND OF THE LIVING

"He was taken from prison and from judgment: and who shall declare his generation? for he was cut off out of the land of the living: for the transgression of my people was he stricken." (**Isaiah 53:8**)

This verse describes the unjust legal proceedings and execution that would befall the Servant. *"He was taken from prison and from judgment"* refers to His arrest and the mockery of justice that characterized His trials. The phrase *"cut off out of the land of the living"* constitutes a clear prophetic reference to His death.

The question *"who shall declare his generation?"* has been interpreted various ways, but in context likely refers to the brevity of His earthly life. Yet the prophet will later reveal that the Servant will *"see his seed"* (**Isaiah 53:10**)—not natural children but spiritual offspring produced through His sacrifice as He brings many sons unto glory (**Hebrews 2:10**).

The verse concludes with another emphatic statement of substitutionary atonement: *"for the transgression of my people was he stricken"*. He died not for His own transgressions but for the rebellions of God's people. The Ethiopian eunuch was reading precisely this verse when Philip found him on the desert road and *"began at the same scripture, and preached unto him Jesus"* (**Acts 8:35**).

BURIED WITH THE WICKED AND RICH

"And he made his grave with the wicked, and with the rich in his death; because he had done no violence, neither was any deceit in his mouth." (**Isaiah 53:9**)

This verse contains a remarkable double prophecy concerning the Messiah's burial circumstances. *"He made his grave with the wicked"* found fulfillment as Jesus was crucified between two thieves, initially destined for the common burial of criminals. *"With the rich in his death"* received its literal fulfillment when Joseph of Arimathea, a wealthy man, provided his own new tomb for Jesus's burial (**Matthew 27:57-60**).

The reason for this treatment follows: *"because he had done no violence, neither was any deceit in his mouth"*. This declaration of absolute sinlessness was essential for the Servant to function as the perfect sacrifice. Unlike every other human being who inherits Adam's sin nature, Jesus *"knew no sin"* (**2 Corinthians 5:21**), was *"a lamb without blemish and without spot"* (**1 Peter 1:19**), and was *"in all points tempted like as we are, yet without sin"* (**Hebrews 4:15**).

THE LORD'S PURPOSE AND ULTIMATE TRIUMPH (ISAIAH 53:10-12)

THE GUILT OFFERING AND RESURRECTION

"Yet it pleased the LORD to bruise him; he hath put him to grief: when thou shalt make his soul an offering for sin, he shall see his seed, he shall prolong his days, and the pleasure of the LORD shall prosper in his hand." (**Isaiah 53:10**)

The phrase *"it pleased the LORD to bruise him"* reveals the godly origin and purpose behind the Servant's suffering. This does not indicate that God delighted in inflicting pain, but rather that the outcome—eternal redemption—brought pleasure to the Father's heart. The suffering was not accidental but essential to God's eternal plan of salvation.

"*When thou shalt make his soul an offering for sin*" refers specifical-ly to the guilt offerings of the Levitical system. Just as these offerings atoned for specific transgressions, the Lamb of God would offer His very soul—His life—as the ultimate guilt offering that would satisfy God's justice once and for all. The substitutionary nature remains clear: He becomes the offering that others deserved to make.

The verse then transitions to resurrection hope: "*he shall see his seed, he shall prolong his days*". Despite being "*cut off from the land of the living,*" the Servant would experience continued life and witness the spiritual offspring produced through His sacrifice. The phrase "*the pleasure of the LORD shall prosper in his hand*" indicates that God's redemptive pur-poses would be successfully accomplished through the Servant's faithful work.

THE RIGHTEOUS SERVANT

"*He shall see of the travail of his soul, and shall be satisfied: by his knowl-edge shall my righteous servant justify many; for he shall bear their iniq-uities.*" (**Isaiah 53:11**)

It pleased the Father to bruise His Son and put Him to grief for you; when His life was offered as a sin offering, the Father would behold the Servant's travail and be satisfied. Our forgiveness flows from the Son's willingness to please the Father through sorrow and travail on our behalf. This satisfaction rests on the faithful obedience and submission of the Son in enduring the cross—His willing bruising constituted the very moment when God's eternal purpose of redemption was carried out.

The declaration, "*by his knowledge shall my righteous servant justify many,*" unveils the means by which a holy God declares unholy sinners to be righteous in His sight. The "*knowledge*" spoken of here is not an intellectual grasp of facts about the Servant; it is a personal, relational, and experiential trust in Him that comes through faith. To be justified is to receive a legal declaration of righteousness from God Himself, not because of any merit in the sinner, but entirely because of the finished work of the "*righteous servant.*" His perfect righteousness is imputed, or credited, to the account of the one who believes. The apostle Paul would later elaborate this Old Testament truth with New Testament clarity: "*Therefore being justified by faith, we have peace with God through our Lord Jesus Christ*" (**Romans 5:1**). The Servant's work on the cross, where He would "*bear their iniquities,*" is the sole basis for this justification. Through faith in His substitutionary death, a sinner's guilt is imputed to Christ, and Christ's righteousness is imputed to the sinner, resulting in a perfect standing before God.

THE TRIUMPHANT REWARD

"*Therefore will I divide him a portion with the great, and he shall divide the spoil with the strong; because he hath poured out his soul unto death: and he was numbered with the transgressors; and he bare the sin of many, and made intercession for the transgressors.*" (**Isaiah 53:12**)

The final verse proclaims the ultimate triumph and vindication of the Suffering Servant. "*Therefore will I divide him a portion with the great*" speaks of the honor and glory bestowed upon the Messiah following His suffering. This was fulfilled in Jesus's resurrection and exaltation to the right hand of the Father, where He now patiently waits the full realization of His complete reward (**Psalm 2**).

"He shall divide the spoil with the strong" employs imagery of a victorious warrior sharing the spoils of battle. This indicates the Messiah's complete victory over sin, death, hell and Satan—a victory shared with His followers who become joint-heirs with Christ. As Alexander MacLaren explained, the Servant becomes *"a conqueror, leading back from His conquests a long train of captives, a rich booty"*.

The basis for this triumph rests upon four accomplishments:

"He hath poured out his soul unto death" - Complete self-giving sacrificial death

"He was numbered with the transgressors" - Identification with sinners (fulfilled at crucifixion)

"He bare the sin of many" - Substitutionary atonement accomplished

"Made intercession for the transgressors" - Ongoing priestly ministry established

This final phrase received fulfillment not only in Jesus's prayer from the cross—*"Father, forgive them; for they know not what they do"* (**Luke 23:34**)—but continues in His present work as our High Priest who *"ever liveth to make intercession for them"* that come unto God by Him (**Hebrews 7:25**).

NEW TESTAMENT FULFILLMENT AND RECOGNITION

Isaiah 53's christological significance permeates the New Testament, demonstrating the apostolic conviction that Jesus perfectly fulfilled these ancient prophecies. The Ethiopian eunuch was reading this very chapter when Philip joined him on the Gaza road, and when asked about the passage's meaning, Philip *"began at the same scripture, and preached unto him Jesus"* (**Acts 8:35**). **Matthew** applied **verse 4** to Jesus's healing ministry (**Matthew 8:17**), **Peter** quoted **verse 5** regarding Christian conduct under persecution (**1 Peter 2:24**), and **Paul** referenced **verse 1** to explain Israel's judicial blindness (**Romans 10:16**).

The precision of these fulfillments confirms that **Isaiah 53** speaks not of Israel's collective suffering or some unnamed individual, but of a specific person—Jesus Christ, the Lamb of God. Every prophetic detail finds completion in the gospel narrative: from His humble origins in Galilee to His silent submission before Pilate, from His crucifixion between thieves to His burial in a rich man's tomb. The mathematical probability of such detailed fulfillment occurring by chance renders coincidence impossible.

IMPLICATIONS FOR THE DISPENSATION OF GRACE

Isaiah 53 establishes several foundational truths that govern Christian doctrine:

Substitutionary Atonement: The chapter's repeated emphasis on *"for our"* and *"in our place"* establishes conclusively that Jesus died as our substitute, bearing the punishment we deserved. This is not moral influence or martyrdom but literal substitution—the innocent bearing the penalty of the guilty. He *"bare our sins in his own body on the tree"* (**1 Peter 2:24**).

Justification by Faith: The Servant's *"knowledge"* justifies many (**verse 11**), pointing directly to the New Testament doctrine of justification by faith apart from works. Jesus *"was delivered for our offences, and was raised again for our justification"* (**Romans 4:25**). The believer's righteousness comes not through personal merit but through faith-union with the righteous Servant.

Eternal Security: The once-for-all nature of the Servant's sacrifice, combined with His ongoing intercession, provides the doctrinal foundation for eternal security. As **Hebrews** says, *"this man, after he had offered one sacrifice for sins for ever, sat down on the right hand of God"* (**Hebrews 10:12**). The work is finished, the price fully paid, the victory complete.

Sanctification: Peter connects the Servant's stripes to holy living, explaining that His suffering enables believers to *"live unto righteousness"* (**1 Peter 2:24**). The liberty purchased by His blood never licenses sin but empowers obedience through the indwelling Spirit.

Isaiah 53 must be understood within the framework of God's dispensational program. The prophet foretold Messiah's rejection by Israel, which opened the parenthetical *"times of the Gentiles"* (**Luke 21:24**). During this present church age, individual Jews and Gentiles alike may receive the benefits of the Servant's atoning work through faith alone in Christ alone.

However, Israel's national acceptance of their Messiah awaits the Second Advent. Paul wrote, *"And so all Israel shall be saved: as it is written, There shall come out of Sion the Deliverer, and shall turn away ungodliness from Jacob"* (**Romans 11:26**). At that time, the kingdom promises will be literally fulfilled, and the Servant who was once despised will be acknowledged as the King of Glory. The same Jesus who came first as the suffering Lamb will return as the conquering Lion of the tribe of Judah.

The present church age exists as God's gracious interval between Messiah's first and second advents. During this time, the benefits of **Isaiah 53's** fulfillment are freely offered to whosoever will believe. Yet this dispensation will conclude with the rapture of the church, followed by **Daniel's** seventieth week and the establishment of Christ's millennial kingdom.

THE PATTERN OF REDEMPTION

Isaiah 53 does not stand in isolation but represents the climactic revelation of a redemptive pattern woven throughout scripture. From the Passover lamb in Egypt to the daily offerings in the temple, every sacrifice pointed forward to this ultimate Lamb. **Genesis 22:8** records Abraham's prophetic declaration: "*God will provide himself a lamb for a burnt offering.*" The Passover lamb of **Exodus 12** prefigured the Lamb whose blood would avert God's wrath. The Levitical offerings detailed in **Leviticus** established the principle that life must be given for life, blood shed for forgiveness.

All these types and shadows found their fulfillment in the Suffering Servant of **Isaiah 53**, which itself still pointed forward to the coming of the Lord Jesus Christ. The progression is clear: promise (**Genesis 3:15**), type (sacrificial system), prophecy (**Isaiah 53**), and fulfillment (Jesus Christ).

THE LAMB TRIUMPHANT

Isaiah 53 concludes not with defeat but with triumph, not with death but with resurrection. The Servant who was "*cut off out of the land of the living*" (**verse 8**) would "*prolong his days*" (**verse 10**) and "*divide the spoil*" *with the strong"* (**verse 12**). His suffering was temporary; His triumph eternal.

The prophet foresaw that the Lord *"shall see of the travail of his soul, and shall be satisfied"* (**verse 11**). This satisfaction comes from the full payment for sin and witnessing the redemption of countless multitudes through His sacrifice. Every sinner saved, every soul redeemed, every believer justified brings joy to the heart of the Lamb who was slain. The Father is satisfied with the work of His Son; the question remains for every reader: **Are you satisfied with the Lamb of God who takes away the sin of the world?**

The Servant's song has been sung; redemption's work is complete. **Isaiah 53** stands forever as God's invitation written in blood, His love letter penned in prophecy, His eternal plan revealed through a suffering Servant who became the triumphant Lamb. Let every redeemed soul echo the worship of heaven: *"Worthy is the Lamb that was slain to receive power, and riches, and wisdom, and strength, and honour, and glory, and blessing"* (**Revelation 5:12**).

For in this ancient prophecy, we behold the very heart of God laid bare—a heart willing to bruise His own Son that He might heal our wounds, willing to forsake His Beloved that He might adopt us as sons, willing to sacrifice the Lamb that He might gather His sheep. **Isaiah 53** is more than prophecy; it is the gospel itself, written in tears and sealed in blood, awaiting only the faith that says, *"Yes, He died, was buried, and rose the third day for me."*

CHAPTER SIX

THE LAMB IN THE DAYS OF HIS FLESH

AN INTRODUCTION TO THE FOUR GOSPELS

A S WE LEAVE BEHIND the shadows and sacrificial systems of the Old Testament, we stand at the commencing point of the most breathtaking narrative ever told: **the fourfold portrait of the Lamb of God in the Gospels**. These four books—**Matthew**, **Mark**, **Luke**, and **John**—are not simple biographies; they are carefully orchestrated revelations, crafted by God to unveil the Lamb from every possible vantage point.

Each Gospel writer, inspired by the Holy Spirit, contributes a unique facet to this portrait. **Matthew** presents the **King**, fulfilling ancient promises; **Mark** unveils the **Servant**, leading in sacrifice; **Luke** portrays the perfect **Man**, embodying compassion; and **John** reveals the eternal **God** who became flesh. Together, they form a harmonious and complete depiction of the Messiah—the Lamb slain from the foundation of the world, now revealed in history and glory.

This chapter invites the reader to journey through these complementary narratives with eyes attuned to dispensational truth and hearts captivated by the Lamb's unfathomable love. We will trace how the Gospels bridge covenantal gaps, unify prophecy and fulfillment, and draw us intimately into the Person and work of the One who "*by himself purged our sins*" (**Hebrews 1:3**).

THE CLIMACTIC DECLARATION

The transition from Old Testament type to New Testament reality reaches its climax in John's Gospel when John the Baptist declares, "*Behold the Lamb of God, which taketh away the sin of the world!*" (**John 1:29**). This profound announcement represents more than introduction—it embodies the fulfillment of millennia of sacrificial typology and prophetic anticipation.

John the Baptist's declaration contains an overt intertextual reference to **Isaiah 53:7**, where the prophet declared He would be "*brought as a lamb to the slaughter*". This prophetic fulfillment demonstrates that **Jesus**, as the Lamb of God, perfectly embodied **Isaiah's** vision of the suffering Servant who would bear our griefs and carry our sorrows. This title appears uniquely in John's Gospel, noting **John's** particular emphasis on Christ's divine nature and sacrificial work.

The term "*Lamb of God*" encompasses the complete Old Testament sacrificial system. **Jesus** fulfills the role of the **daily tamid sacrifice** that was offered twice daily—'*one lamb in the morning and one lamb in the evening*' at the **third hour** (*9 AM*) and **ninth hour** (*3 PM*). Significantly, **Jesus** was crucified at the **third hour** (*9 AM*) and died at **3 PM**, the exact time of the evening sacrifice (**Matthew 27:45-50, Mark 15:25-37**).

THE FOUR GOSPELS AS TRANSITIONAL LITERATURE

UNDERSTANDING THE DISPENSATIONAL FRAMEWORK

The Four Gospels occupy a unique position as **transitional books** that bridge Old Testament law and New Testament grace. In these sacred accounts, the reader witnesses two great movements occurring simultaneously: **the closing of the Old Testament as Christ perfectly fulfills its every jot and tittle, and the dawning of the New Testament, which would be consummated by His death on the cross.** This transitional nature creates interpretive challenges when Old and New Testament doctrines exist side by side within the same narrative.

According to **Hebrews 9:16-17**, a testament is of force only after the death of the testator. This means the New Testament, did not formally begin until Christ's death on the cross. Consequently, much of the Gospel material, including the ministry of the Lord Jesus, occurs under the Old Testament dispensation, even as He introduces the principles of the New.

This dispensational understanding is crucial for proper interpretation. When Jesus instructed the healed leper to "*show himself to the priest, and offer for thy cleansing those things which Moses commanded*" (**Mark 1:44**), He was operating under Old Testament law, demonstrating His perfect submission to the very law He came to fulfill. Such passages require careful dispensational analysis to avoid confusing the requirements of the Law with the realities of the grace that would be established by His blood.

The Gospels and Israel's Program

From a dispensational perspective, the Gospels (primarily **Matthew**) record God's offer of the Kingdom to Israel through their Messiah. Jesus came *"unto his own, and his own received him not"* (**John 1:11**), culminating in national rejection. This understanding helps explain why certain Gospel passages seem inconsistent with **New Testament** church doctrine—they were addressing Israel under different dispensational principles. Rightly Dividing the word of truth requires that we carefully distinguish between **Israel** and **the Church**, recognizing they are **distinct entities** with **separate programs** in God's plan—they are neither the same nor do they replace one another.

FOUR DISTINCT PERSPECTIVES OF THE ONE LAMB

God's Orchestration of Four Accounts

Why did God provide four Gospel accounts rather than one comprehensive narrative? The answer lies in the multifaceted nature of Christ Himself and the complete revelation required to understand His person and work. Consider the four Gospels as four vantage points—north, south, east, and west—each illuminating a distinct facet of the one Lamb of God, so that together they form a complete, four-dimensional portrait of His person and work.

Each Gospel was written to a different audience with specific needs:

Matthew: Written to Jews, emphasizing Jesus as the promised Messiah and King

Mark: Written to Romans, emphasizing Jesus as the dutiful Servant

Luke: Written to Greeks, emphasizing Jesus as the perfect Man

John: Written to all men everywhere, emphasizing Jesus as God incarnate

A Bible-Believing Rejection of the "Synoptic Problem"

In approaching the Four Gospels, it is essential to fortify our minds against the encroachments of secular academia, which, under a pretense of objectivity, often seeks to dismantle the authority of scripture. A primary example of this is the so-called "Synoptic Problem," a man-made theory that has dominated critical scholarship for over a century.

This theory uses the term *"synoptic"* (meaning *"to see together"* or *"a single view"*) to improperly group **Matthew, Mark**, and **Luke**, suggesting they are so alike that they must have copied from one another or a lost source, while treating **John's** Gospel as a theological outlier. This approach is born from a refusal to accept the divine inspiration of scripture. It presumes that the Bible must be subjected to the same literary criticism as any human book, thereby dismissing the Holy Spirit as the ultimate author.

We, however, reject such reasoning. A Bible-believing approach does not begin with a *"problem"* to be solved but with a divine revelation to be received. The assertion that three of the four Gospels are so similar that they merit being isolated from the fourth is disingenuous. In truth, **Matthew, Mark, and Luke are just as different from one another as they are similar**, and **John's** Gospel shares numerous commonalities with the other three. The very premise of the *"synoptic problem"* is flawed because it magnifies similarities to invent a literary dependency while ignoring the profound, God-ordained differences that give each Gospel its unique power and purpose.

The differences between the Gospels are not a problem; **they are the solution**. They are the evidence of God's perfect design to present a complete, four-dimensional portrait of His Son. Where the world sees a literary puzzle, the believer sees a divine gallery, with four masterpieces revealing the glory of the one Lamb of God from four distinct vantage points:

Matthew presents Christ as the **King**.

Mark presents Christ as the **Servant**.

Luke presents Christ as the **Son of Man**.

John presents Christ as the **Son of God**.

These are not competing narratives but **complementary testimonies**. To suggest that one is more or less historical, or that some are merely derivative of another, is to miss the Spirit's intention entirely. We do not need a hypothetical "Q" document or a complex web of literary borrowing to explain the Gospels. We need only to believe that God, in His infinite wisdom, moved upon four different men to record four perfect and distinct accounts, each tailored to reveal a specific facet of the character and work of the Lord Jesus Christ. Our commitment is to honor the Bible's manifest unity and its glorious diversity, trusting that these four God-breathed accounts serve His eternal purpose with intended richness.

THE FOUR PERSPECTIVES DEFINED

Matthew presents Christ as KING. This Gospel begins with the genealogy establishing Jesus as *"the son of David, the son of Abraham"* (**Matthew 1:1**), immediately connecting Him to the Davidic covenant and Abrahamic promises. **Matthew** contains more Old Testament quotations than any other Gospel (**62 direct quotations plus 262 allusions**), demonstrating how Jesus fulfills Messianic prophecy. **Matthew's** focus on the **PAST** helps demonstrate how Jesus fulfills Old Testament expectations.

Mark presents Christ as SERVANT. This Gospel contains no genealogy because servants don't require pedigrees. **Mark** emphasizes Jesus' actions rather than His teachings, showing the Servant who *"came not to be ministered unto, but to minister, and to give his life a ransom for many"* (**Mark 10:45**). The focus is on the **PRESENT**—immediate action and service.

Luke presents Christ as the perfect MAN. **Luke** traces Jesus' genealogy back to Adam (**Luke 3:38**), establishing His connection to all humanity. This Gospel emphasizes Christ's compassion for the poor, outcasts, and Gentiles, showing Him as the ideal representative of the human race. The focus is on the **FUTURE**—hope for all people.

John presents Christ as GOD. Beginning with *"In the beginning was the Word, and the Word was with God, and the Word was God"* (**John 1:1**), this Gospel emphasizes Christ's eternal deity and divine nature. This Gospel presents several conversations in which the Lord declares to the Jews that He is the Son of God. John's focus is on **ETERNITY**—Christ's eternal existence and divine attributes.

These truths, expressed in four distinct portraits, are not contradictory but complementary, and each is necessary to appreciate fully who Jesus Christ is. Just as a man can be simultaneously a father, a son, a husband, and a professional in his career, so the four Gospels reveal different, yet equally true, dimensions of our Lord's person and work. To ask which one is the "real" Jesus is to ask a flawed question. To receive a complete revelation, one must embrace all four portraits of the Lamb who is at once King, Servant, Man, and God.

OLD TESTAMENT FOUNDATIONS FOR THE FOUR PERSPECTIVES

THE CHERUBIM VISION IN EZEKIEL

The Four Gospel perspectives find remarkable **Old Testament** support in **Ezekiel's** vision of the cherubim with four faces: "*the face of a man, and the face of a lion, and the face of an ox, and the face of an eagle*" (**Ezekiel 1:10**).

This imagery from Ezekiel's vision, recognized by the Church since its earliest days, finds its majestic parallel in the four Evangelists' distinct portrayals of our Lord:

The face of a man, emblematic of **Luke**, reveals the perfect Man, our gracious and compassionate Redeemer.

The face of a lion, resonant with **Matthew**, proclaims the King, whose authority resounds like the roaring lion (**Proverbs 19:12**).

The face of an ox, humble and strong, aligns with **Mark's** vision of the Servant, bearing our burdens along the path of perfect obedience (**1 Timothy 5:18**).

The face of an eagle, lofty and piercing, corresponds with **John,** soaring on divine wings and beholding the eternal with God-like vision and insight (**Proverbs 23:5**).

Together, these four divinely inspired faces add to the tapestry of truth, each perspective indispensable, weaving a complete and glorious panorama of the Messiah's person and work. They invite us into a fuller, deeper adoration of the Lamb who was slain, yet lives and reigns forevermore.

THE FOUR BRANCH PROPHECIES

To further bolster this truth, the **Old Testament** contains four distinct prophecies using the word *"Branch"* that correspond perfectly to the Four Gospel presentations:

Jeremiah 23:5-6 proclaims, *"I will raise unto David a righteous **Branch**; and a **King** shall reign,"* attuned to the regal majesty presented in **Matthew's** Gospel.

Zechariah 3:8 declares, *"Behold, I will bring forth my **Servant**, the **Branch**,"* unfolding the devoted servant rendered in **Mark's** account.

Zechariah 6:12 reveals, *"Behold the **man** whose name is the **Branch**,"* reflecting the perfect man glorified in **Luke's** narrative.

Isaiah 4:2 foretells, *"The **Branch of the LORD** shall be beautiful and glorious,"* resonant with the deity unveiled in **John's** testimony.

This prophetic pattern, intricately woven throughout the text, attests not to happenstance but to the careful orchestration of Almighty God — a glorious demonstration of unity and diversity in the revelation of the Lamb of God.

THE TABERNACLE VEIL

FROM BARRIER TO WELCOME

In **Exodus 26:31–32** we behold a veil of exquisite workmanship, woven of blue, purple, and scarlet, embroidered with cherubim, and suspended upon **four acacia pillars**—each overlaid with pure gold. For centuries that curtain stood as a sobering reminder of man's estrangement from God's presence, barring all but the high priest—once each year—under the weight of solemn atonement, lest he perish in the unapproachable holiness beyond.

Yet at Calvary, when **Christ gave up the ghost**, the very veil of separation was sundered *"from the top to the bottom,"* not by human hands but by the hand of God Himself (**Matthew 27:51**). In that single rending event, the barrier that had so long proclaimed judgment became the testimony of mercy—an open gateway inviting sinners, by faith, to draw near.

THE VEIL OF HIS FLESH

Hebrews 10:19–20 unveils the profound symbolism: *"Having therefore, brethren, boldness to enter into the holiest by the blood of Jesus, by a new and living way, which he hath consecrated for us, through the veil, that is to say, his flesh."* Here the incarnate Son becomes the very veil—His flesh—transforming exclusion into access, judgment into welcome, and death into life. Where once only the High Priest might tread with trembling foot, now every repentant heart may enter with boldness into the holiest by the blood of Jesus, clothed not in ritual garments but in the redeeming efficacy of His shed blood.

THE FOUR GOSPEL PILLARS

Just as four golden pillars once upheld the veil of the earthly tabernacle, separating sinful man from a holy God, so the Four Gospels (**Matthew, Mark, Luke, John**) lift up the Lord with four clear pillars, upholding the greater reality of *"the veil, that is to say, his flesh"* (**Hebrews 10:20**). Each Gospel writer, inspired by the Holy Ghost, presents a unique and indispensable portrait of the Lord Jesus Christ. Together, they provide a complete and unassailable testimony to the Lamb of God, who alone grants us access into the holiest of all.

THE FOURFOLD TESTIMONY OF THE GOSPELS

Matthew: The Messiah and King

In the Gospel of **Matthew**, we are met with the majestic and authoritative person of the Messiah and King. This portrait is not of a teacher, but of the long-awaited Messiah, whose right to the throne of Israel is established with irrefutable, authority.

First, Matthew establishes Christ's **legal right** through His royal lineage, beginning his Gospel with the genealogy that meticulously traces Jesus' descent from Abraham through King David, the rightful heir to the throne. This is His birthright. **Second, Matthew** establishes Christ's **prophetic right**, weaving throughout his narrative a rich tapestry of fulfilled Old Testament prophecies. Each miracle, each sermon, and each action serves as another credential, another proof that He is indeed the Christ, the Messiah foretold by the prophets.

Therefore, His authority is absolute. His commands are not suggestions but royal edicts, and His power over disease, devils, and death itself validates His claim to the throne. Yet, the supreme paradox of this King is that He exercises His ultimate authority not by seizing power, but by laying down His life, submitting to the cross before He reigns from a throne.

Mark: The Suffering Servant

Mark's Gospel presents a portrait in stark contrast, yet perfectly complementary. Here, we see the Lord not on a throne, but in the posture of a **servant**. Mark's account is one of ceaseless activity; the word "straightway" appears repeatedly, painting a picture of a man driven by mission and service. He is the Suffering Servant of **Isaiah**, come *"not to be ministered unto, but to minister, and to give his life a ransom for many"* (**Mark 10:45**). The emphasis is not on what He said, but on what He did. His hands, which healed the sick and blessed children, were the hands of a servant, and ultimately, they were pierced for our transgressions.

Luke: The Perfect Man

The Gospel of **Luke** offers a deeply human and relatable portrait of Christ as the Perfect Man. **Luke**, the beloved physician, emphasizes His **compassion**. We see a Savior who is moved by the plight of the outcast, the poor, and the sorrowful. It is in **Luke** that we find the tender truths of the Good Samaritan and the Prodigal Son. He is presented as the Son of Man, embodying the ideal of humanity—sinless, yet full of grace and empathy. This is the High Priest who can be "*touched with the feeling of our infirmities*" (**Hebrews 4:15**), because He walked among us, sharing in our sorrows, yet without sin.

John: The Eternal Word Incarnate

Finally, **John's** Gospel soars into the heavenlies, presenting Christ in His full **divinity**. **John** begins not with a genealogy or a flurry of activity, but in eternity past: "*In the beginning was the Word, and the Word was with God, and the Word was God*" (**John 1:1**). The emphasis here is on the divine nature of the Lord Jesus. He is the eternal Son, the Creator of all things, veiled in human flesh. John records the great "*I AM*" statements, where Christ takes upon Himself the very name of Jehovah. This is the Lamb of God, whose origin is not of this world, and whose sacrifice therefore has eternal and infinite value.

Together, these four portraits—Messiah and King, Sacrificial Service, Empathetic Compassion, and Eternal Divinity—unite to form a complete and harmonious testimony of our Lord Jesus Christ. Far from conflicting, they are carefully orchestrated to complement one another, each shedding light on an essential facet of His person and redemptive work. Through this multifaceted witness, believers behold the Lamb revealed behind the veil, and are invited to enter boldly into everlasting fellowship with the living God. As the Lord said, "*I am the way, the truth, and the life*" (**John 14:6**), so it is by embracing the fullness of these testimonies that the way of salvation is fully revealed.

INVITATION TO DRAW NEAR

The veil no longer warns, "*Keep out.*" It beckons, "*Come.*" Every repentant sinner may now approach the throne of grace with bold assurance, abandoning self-righteousness and trusting wholly in Christ's finished work **(John 1:39, John 4:25-40, Revelation 22:17)**.

Thus what was the privilege of one man once a year has become the everyday inheritance of all who believe: **uninhibited communion with God through the veil—Jesus, the Lamb of God who saves sinners.**

FROM MULTIPLE SACRIFICES TO THE ONE SACRIFICE

Throughout the Old Testament, the progression of lamb sacrifices reveals God's redemptive plan:

Genesis 22: One lamb for one person (Isaac)

Exodus 12: One lamb for one household (Passover)

Leviticus 16: One sacrifice for one nation (Day of Atonement)

John 1:29: One Lamb for the whole world

This progression demonstrates how God's redemptive plan expanded from individual to universal scope, culminating in Christ as *"the Lamb of God, which taketh away the sin of the world."*

PRACTICAL APPLICATION FOR UNDERSTANDING THE GOSPELS

DISPENSATIONAL READING PRINCIPLES

When approaching the Four Gospels with proper understanding of the Lamb of God theme, several principles emerge:

Recognize the transitional nature: Gospel events occur primarily under Old Testament dispensation until Christ's death

Understand the audience: Each Gospel addresses specific groups with particular needs and a specific overall emphasis

See the complementary perspectives: The four views together provide complete revelation

Connection to Old Testament types: Gospel narratives fulfill sacrificial and prophetic patterns

Maintain the Lamb focus: Every Gospel ultimately points to Christ as the sacrificial Lamb

THE CENTRAL UNIFYING TRUTH

The truth that unifies all Four Gospel perspectives is found in **1 Timothy 2:5**: *"For there is one God, and one mediator between God and men, the man Christ Jesus"* This verse encompasses all four presentations—Christ as the Messiah-King, perfect Servant, ideal Man, and eternal Mediator. Each Gospel contributes essential elements to our complete understanding of the Lamb of God.

THE COMPLETE REVELATION

The Four Gospels function together as a carefully orchestrated revelation of Jesus Christ as the Lamb of God. From John the Baptist's initial declaration to Revelation's eternal worship of the Lamb, these four accounts provide the complete bridge from Old Testament anticipation to New Testament fulfillment.

The Four Gospels are not only historical accounts—they are scriptural portraits that reveal different facets of the one Lamb of God who takes away the sin of the world. Through proper dispensational interpretation and recognition of their transitional nature, these books become powerful testimonies to the complete person and work of Christ, perfectly fulfilling every **Old Testament** type and prophecy while establishing the foundation for New Testament doctrine.

CHAPTER SEVEN

THE PERSON, THE LAMB

John 1:29-36 will mark the pivotal transition from shadow to substance as John the Baptist publicly identifies Jesus as *"the Lamb of God which taketh away the sin of the world"* —the moment when prophecy stepped into history.

THE GRAND VESTIBULE

JOHN 1:29 *"BEHOLD THE Lamb of God, which taketh away the sin of the world."* The first chapter of John's Gospel is scripture's grand vestibule, where all the scattered streams of redemptive history converge in perfect unity. The eternal **Word** who *"was with God, and was God"* (**John 1:1**) and *"by whom all things were made"* (**John 1:3**) steps from unsearchable glory into human history, becoming *"flesh"* (**John 1:14**) to dwell among men. In this remarkable chapter, every pre-Christian type finds its glorious fulfillment, and every subsequent New Testament truth concerning the Lamb draws its foundation.

Here, Abraham's ancient cry from Mount Moriah—*"God will provide himself a lamb for a burnt offering"* (**Genesis 22:8**)—receives its answer. The daily sacrifices that ascended morning and evening from Israel's altars, those countless lambs whose blood flowed continually at the prescribed times, all pointed forward to this moment. The Passover lamb, slain *"between the two evenings"* (**Exodus 12:6**) and whose blood protected God's people from death, finds its ultimate reality in Him who would die at the very hour when Jerusalem's Passover lambs were being slain. Every sin offering prescribed by Moses, every burnt offering that ascended as a *"sweet savour"* unto the Lord, every ceremonial cleansing—all gathered their meaning from this Lamb of whom John testified.

The chapter presents Christ as both the eternal God who created all things and the sacrifice who would die for all men, identifying Him as the perfect Kinsman-Redeemer who bridges the infinite gulf between God's holiness and man's need through His substitutionary death. John the Baptist's repeated declaration—first the comprehensive *"Behold the Lamb of God, which taketh away the sin of the world"* (**John 1:29**), then the simpler yet more emphatic *"Behold the Lamb of God!"* (**John 1:36**)—marks the pivotal transition from shadow to substance, from type to antitype, from promise to fulfillment.

In this grand vestibule, prophecy stepped into history, and the Lamb slain from the foundation of the world stood ready to accomplish that eternal redemption for which all previous lambs had been but temporary, preparatory shadows.

THE ETERNAL WORD IN GLORY (JOHN 1:1-5)

John's prologue lifts the reader beyond the realm of time and space into the eternal councils of the Godhead. The opening declaration, *"In the beginning was the Word, and the Word was with God, and the Word was*

God" (**John 1:1**), establishes three foundational truths that undergird successive revelation about Christ as the Lamb of God.

First, the verse establishes His **eternal existence**. The phrase, *"In the beginning **was** the Word,"* does not signify a starting point for the Word, but rather declares His continuous being. When creation itself had a beginning, the Word already existed. This enforces the doctrine of His pre-existence, confirming that He is not a created being but is outside and above the confines of time.

Second, the Apostle John makes clear His **personal distinction**. The statement, *"and the Word was **with** God,"* reveals a relationship of intimate communion between two distinct persons. The Word is not an impersonal attribute or emanation of the Father, but a Person in fellowship *with* the Father. This guards against the error of modalism, which confuses the Persons of the Godhead, and establishes the eternal relationship between the Father and the Son.

Third, the verse unequivocally affirms His **full Deity**. The climactic phrase, *"and the Word **was** God,"* leaves no room for doubt or compromise regarding His divine nature. It does not say He was *like* God or *a* god, but that He, the Word, possessed the very essence and nature of God. This truth, that the Word who *"was made flesh, and dwelt among us"* (**John 1:14**) is fully God, is the bedrock of our salvation, for only a divine sacrifice could atone for the sins of the world.

From that lofty height of eternal glory, the Lord descends to creation itself: *"All things were made by him; and without him was not any thing made that was made"* (**John 1:3**). This comprehensive declaration establishes that the Word is **both Architect and Sustainer** of every molecule in existence. As Creator, He brought all things into being; as

Sustainer, "*by him all things consist*" (**Colossians 1:17**), and He upholds "*all things by the word of his power*" (**Hebrews 1:3**).

The Word who would become the sacrificial Lamb is none other than the eternal God who spoke reality into existence, the One "*in whom we live, and move, and have our being*" (**Acts 17:28**). This foundation proves essential to understanding the infinite value of His atoning sacrifice—only the Creator of all life could give His life as a ransom for all (**1 Timothy 2:6**).

THE PERSONAL DISTINCTION OF THE WORD

When John declares that "*The Word was with God,*" he presents a truth of magnificent weight, framed in the simplest of terms. The word "*with*" is one of relation, not of solitude. A man cannot be *with* himself; the term inherently requires at least two distinct persons. Therefore, the Holy Spirit immediately establishes that The Word is a Person, eternally distinct from God the Father. They are not one and the same Person, but two.

However, this distinction does not imply separation or inferiority. Instead, it speaks of an intimate, unbroken communion. It is the language of fellowship, of a face-to-face relationship marked by perfect harmony and shared purpose. The Word was not simply located near God, but existed in a perpetual bond of love and glory with the Father.

This foundational truth is what gives the sacrifice of the Lamb its profound and personal power. Our redemption was not accomplished by an abstract, solitary God. Rather, it was a transaction of infinite love within the Godhead itself. The Son, as a distinct Person, willingly offered Himself *to* the Father, the very One with whom He had shared eternal fellowship. Salvation, therefore, is not the result of an impersonal force, but is anchored in the voluntary sacrifice of the Lamb, offered by the Son to the Father in an eternal act of love for mankind.

THE FULL DEITY OF THE WORD

With the declaration, *"and the Word was God,"* John brings us to the summit of this majestic introduction. This is not a description of a lesser god or a secondary power, but a statement of absolute being. The Word did not simply possess divine qualities; He *was* God in His very nature and essence. His being is co-equal and co-eternal with that of the Father.

This truth is the bedrock upon which our salvation is built. If the Lamb of God were anything less than God Himself, His sacrifice would be finite and insufficient. A creature cannot redeem another creature from the judgment of an infinite Creator. Only God could satisfy the demands of His own perfect holiness and justice. Therefore, the infinite value of the atonement rests entirely upon the infinite nature of the One who atoned. It was God, manifest in the flesh, who shed His own blood for the sins of the world.

Herein lies a sacred mystery that we must receive by faith: there is only one true and living God, yet He exists eternally in three distinct Persons—the Father, the Word (who is the Son), and the Holy Ghost. To know God rightly is to honor this truth. One cannot claim to worship the Father while denying the Son, for Jesus Himself declared, *"he that honoureth not the Son honoureth not the Father which hath sent him"* (**John 5:23**). Our worship must be directed to the one God who is Father, Son, and Holy Ghost. It is this very Word, the eternal Son of God, who took upon Himself the form of a man, so that as Jesus Christ, He could become the perfect Lamb slain for the sins of the world.

"All things were made by him; and without him was not any thing made that was made" (**John 1:3**) establishes the Word as the active agent in creation. Every molecule, every atom, every star owes its existence to Him who would later become *"the Lamb slain from the foundation of the world"* (**Revelation 13:8**). The Creator becoming the sacrifice represents the ultimate reversal—He who spoke earth into existence would yield His life to redeem His creation.

LIGHT AND DARKNESS IN CONFLICT

In the profound declaration, *"In him was life; and the life was the light of men. And the light shineth in darkness; and the darkness comprehended it not"* (**John 1:4-5**), the Holy Spirit lays bare the great spiritual state of the world with a precision that is at once majestic and solemn. Here is not a battle of competing powers, but the serene and steady shining of light into darkness that is utterly oblivious to its presence.

The life described is God's own—uncreated and eternal. This life becomes the light for men, an illuminating principle in a world that has, through its own devices, fallen into a pervasive and pitiable blindness. The tragedy unfolds in the final clause: the darkness *"comprehended it not."* This is a failure of perception, a profound spiritual ignorance. The darkness, which is the settled state of the fallen human mind, is so complete, so self-satisfied in its own shadows, that when the very source of all truth and reality shines upon it, it has no faculty with which to recognize it. It is like describing colour to a man born blind; the words are heard, but the reality is entirely missed.

The Apostle, guided by the Spirit, does not permit us to wander into speculation on this point. He provides his own immediate commentary, confirming that the issue is one of tragic non-recognition: "*He was in the world, and the world was made by him, and the world knew him not*" (**John 1:10**). The Creator walked among His own creation, the architect through His own halls, and yet He was met with the vacant stare of ignorance. Therefore, the great conflict established here is not one of physical force, but of spiritual reality versus spiritual blindness. It is the majestic, unwavering light of God shining upon the heart of man, a heart so darkened by its own state that it simply cannot see the glory in its midst, demonstrating the profound depth of our need for the Holy Spirit to open our eyes.

THE FORERUNNER'S WITNESS (JOHN 1:6-8, 15-28)

A MAN SENT FROM GOD

"*There was a man sent from God, whose name was John*" (**John 1:6**). The simplicity of this statement belies its profound significance. John the Baptist emerges as the final voice of the Old Testament prophetic tradition, the bridge between law and grace, the herald who would identify the promised Lamb. His mission was singular: "*to bear witness of that Light, that all men through him might believe*" (**John 1:7**).

John's humility shines forth in his clear declaration: "*He was not that Light, but was sent to bear witness of that Light*" (**John 1:8**). In an age when religious leaders sought prominence and recognition, John consistently pointed away from himself to the greater One coming after him. His self-effacing attitude becomes the model for all who would proclaim the Lamb of God—we are but voices crying in the wilderness, heralds of the Lamb.

TESTIMONY BEFORE THE DELEGATION

When religious authorities from Jerusalem questioned John's identity and authority (**John 1:19-28**), he consistently deflected attention from himself. He denied being the Christ, Elijah, or "*that prophet,*" identifying himself only as "*the voice of one crying in the wilderness, Make straight the way of the Lord*" (**John 1:23**). This echo from **Isaiah 40:3** positioned John as the herald preparing the way for the Lord's visitation.

The questioners pressed further, asking why he baptized if he claimed no special identity (**John 1:25**). John's response reveals his understanding of his temporal mission: "*I baptize with water: but there standeth one among you, whom ye know not; He it is, who coming after me is preferred before me, whose shoe's latchet I am not worthy to unloose*" (**John 1:26-27**). The Lamb of God was already present among them, though unrecognized by the religious establishment.

THE WORD MADE FLESH (JOHN 1:9-14)

THE TRUE LIGHT COMES

"*That was the true Light, which lighteth every man that cometh into the world*" (**John 1:9**). The Word who existed in eternal glory with the Father now enters the realm of time and space as the "*true Light*". This entrance represents the greatest condescension in history—the infinite becoming finite, the eternal entering time, the Creator becoming part of His creation.

The tragedy of man's blindness unfolds in stark terms: *"He was in the world, and the world was made by him, and the world knew him not. He came unto his own, and his own received him not"* (**John 1:10-11**). The creation failed to recognize its Creator. His own people, to whom He had revealed Himself through centuries of covenant relationship, rejected their promised Messiah. This rejection would ultimately lead to the cross, where the world's love for darkness and hatred of the light would be fully revealed.

Yet not all rejected the Light: *"But as many as received him, to them gave he power to become the sons of God, even to them that believe on his name"* (**John 1:12**). The word *"power"* indicates authority or right and ability. Those who receive Christ are given power *"to become"* - this is an essential reality to understand. This new birth *"not of blood, nor of the will of the flesh, nor of the will of man, but of God"* (**John 1:13**) emphasizes its godly origin and supernatural character. We are not born into Christianity, we must **become** the sons of God by receiving, believing, trusting Jesus Christ.

THE INCARNATION

"And the Word became flesh, and dwelt among us, (and we beheld his glory, the glory as of the only begotten of the Father,) full of grace and truth" (**John 1:14**). This verse unveils the greatest miracle in history: the eternal Word—the unoriginate One who *"was in the beginning with God"*—**took upon Himself complete human nature**. The phrase *"the Word became"* marks a singular moment in time when the timeless entered our time, and the infinite clothed Himself in our finitude. In this, we behold a mystery of marvellous symmetry: the same power which grants fallen men the right to *become* the sons of God is reverse engi-

neered so that the eternal Son of God condescended to *become* the Son of man.

The term *"dwelt among us"* recalls the tabernacle where God's glory hovered over Israel in the wilderness. Yet here the presence is far more intimate: the Word pitched His tent in human flesh, walking dusty roads, dining at peasant tables, and touching leprous skin. The *"glory"* they beheld was not the consuming fire of Sinai, which would have scorched mortal eyes, but a glory veiled in humility—*the only begotten of the Father, full of grace and truth.*

The coupling of **grace and truth** in the Incarnation unites two essential realities that would otherwise stand in irreconcilable tension. Truth, by its very nature, exposes sin, pronounces guilt, and would be man's unmitigated downfall. Under the law, God's truth stood as an immovable mirror, reflecting every transgression and leaving no room for self-justification. The Mosaic code imposed demands (*"Thou shalt"* and *"Thou shalt not..."*), yet offered no power to obey, no remedy for the sinner it revealed.

Grace, however, extends a merciful pause—a space in which the condemned may turn from false hope and face reality. By surrounding truth with grace, Christ provides both the conviction of sin and the power to repent. In Him, the unrelenting demands of truth do not crush the penitent but lead them into a deeper appreciation of mercy. Grace becomes the enabling environment in which truth can transform, rather than destroy, the human heart.

"For the law was given by Moses, but grace and truth came by Jesus Christ" (**John 1:17**). In Christ, grace and truth meet seamlessly: grace forgives the guilty, truth restores the broken. Christ brings both **mercy and**

might—mercy to forgive our failures and might to transform our hearts. At the cross, the Lamb of God bore the full penalty of truth and poured forth the boundless riches of grace, satisfying God's justice while opening the way for guilty souls to approach God without condemnation.

Moreover, grace and truth point us forward to Christ's ultimate declaration: "*I am the way, the truth, and the life*" (**John 14:6**). Only through His sacrificial work can truth be fully embraced without despair, and only by His unmerited favor can sinners embark upon the path He has opened. In the Lamb of God, truth no longer stands as an obstacle but as a beacon guiding weary souls into fullness of life. Grace no longer simply pardons the guilty but empowers them to walk in the way of holiness revealed by that same truth.

In the Incarnation, then, we see **godly condescension** that preserves God's holiness while extending His mercy. The Word became flesh not to erase His deity, **but to enflesh His grace**, making salvation both accessible and certain. This is no simplistic example of humility; it is the once-for-all act by which the **Lamb of God**, in infinite love, united Himself to our humanity that He might bear our sins, reconcile us to the Father, and shine in us as the true Light of the world. Grace and truth together are not concessions to human weakness but the very means by which God's holiness and love coexist, inviting all who believe into the eternal fellowship of the Father, the Son, and the Spirit.

THE CLIMACTIC PROCLAMATION (JOHN 1:29-34)

THE HERALD'S GREATEST HOUR

"The next day John seeth Jesus coming unto him, and saith, Behold the Lamb of God, which taketh away the sin of the world" (**John 1:29**). This moment represents the climax of John's ministry and the pinnacle of Old Testament revelation. In identifying Jesus as *"the Lamb of God,"* John crystallized centuries of sacrificial typology into one living Person. In essence, the Law just brought you to Christ!

The title "Lamb of God" contains certain profound truths:

God's Provision: The Lamb is *"of God"*—not provided by man but by God Himself. Abraham's prophetic words to Isaac, *"God will provide himself a lamb for a burnt offering"* (**Genesis 22:8**), finds clear fulfillment in Christ. What human effort could never supply, God's grace freely provides.

Sacrificial Character: The lamb imagery immediately evokes sacrifice. Every faithful Jew would think of the morning and evening sacrifices, the Passover lamb, the Day of Atonement offerings. All these pointed forward to the one great sacrifice that would end the need for all others.

Innocence and Purity: Lambs represent innocence, gentleness, and purity. The sacrificial laws required animals *"without blemish"* (**Exodus 12:5**), prefiguring the moral perfection of Christ. Peter later described Him as *"a lamb without blemish and without spot"* (**1 Peter 1:19**).

Substitutionary Atonement: The lamb dies in the place of the guilty. Every sacrificial lamb pointed to the great substitution where Christ would bear the penalty of sin on behalf of sinners.

THE "SIN OF THE WORLD"

John declares that this Lamb *"taketh away the sin of the world"*. Jesus Christ would take the sins of the world and carry them away, or remove them completely. Christ doesn't simply cover sin temporarily like Old Testament sacrifices, but removes it entirely. The scope is universal—*"the sin of the world"*—encompassing all humanity in every age.

The singular *"sin"* rather than *"sins"* points to sin as a principle, a nature, a condition, rather than individual acts. Christ addresses not just the symptoms but man's root disease. His sacrifice deals with both the guilt of sin and its power over human hearts.

John's testimony continues with the authentication he had witnessed at Christ's baptism: *"And John bare record, saying, I saw the Spirit descending from heaven like a dove, and it abode upon him"* (**John 1:32**).

This visible manifestation of the Holy Spirit served multiple purposes:

Identification of the Messiah: God had revealed to John that the One upon whom he saw the Spirit descend would be the Messiah. This sign confirmed beyond doubt that Jesus was the promised Messiah.

Anointing for Ministry: The Spirit's descent anointed Jesus to preach and teach on earth. **Luke** records that Jesus was *"anointed with the Holy Ghost and with power"* (**Acts 10:38, Luke 4:18**).

Trinitarian Witness: The baptismal scene reveals all three Persons of the Trinity—the Father's voice from heaven, the Son in the water, and the Spirit descending like a dove. This trinitarian witness (**1 John 5:7**) validates Jesus as the Son of God.

Prophetic Fulfillment: Isaiah prophesied that the Spirit would rest upon the Messiah (**Isaiah 11:2; 61:1**). The visible descent fulfilled these ancient prophecies.

THE GREATER BAPTISM

John the Baptist's ministry foreshadowed a deeper washing than the waters of the Jordan. "*I indeed baptize you with water unto repentance*" (**Matthew 3:11**), he declared, yet he looked forward to Christ's superior work. "*And I knew him not: but he that sent me to baptize with water, the same said unto me, Upon whom thou shalt see the Spirit descending, and remaining on him, the same is he which baptizeth with the Holy Ghost.*" (**John 1:33**). John's baptism was preparatory and external, reserved for those who bore "*fruits meet for repentance*" (**Matthew 3:8**). Only when one's heart had turned did he immerse them as a public testimony of sin forgiven and life to follow.

In the early church this order persisted. When the Ethiopian eunuch asked Philip, "*See, here is water; what doth hinder me to be baptized?*" Philip answered, "*If thou believest with all thine heart,*" and the eunuch replied, "*I believe that Jesus Christ is the Son of God,*" before receiving water baptism (**Acts 8:36–37**). This clear sequence—faith first, then Spirit baptism, and finally water baptism—was never intended to elevate the ordinance of water above the inward work of grace and trust in Christ.

Far greater is the baptism administered by the risen Lord Himself. "*For by one Spirit are we all baptized into one body*" (**1 Corinthians 12:13**). The moment a sinner trusts Christ, the Spirit unites that soul to the body of Christ, indwelling, sealing, and empowering them for holy living (**Eph-**

esians 1:13–14). This baptism is permanent and internal, producing regeneration, imparting gifts, and sealing the believer unto the day of redemption.

Thus, water baptism remains a solemn, outward witness to the inward change wrought by grace, but it must never be elevated above Spirit baptism. The Lamb of God, having died as the substitute for our sins and risen in victory, now baptizes with the Holy Spirit—bestowing life, power, and union with Himself. Water baptism points backward to repentance and cleansing; Spirit baptism secures our place in Christ and propels us forward into His likeness. Only by maintaining this biblical order can the believer honour both in their proper place: water as confession and Spirit as transformation.

THE FIRSTFRUITS OF FAITH (JOHN 1:35-51)

THE FIRST DISCIPLES CALLED

Following John's second proclamation of Jesus as *"the Lamb of God"* (**John 1:36**), two of his disciples immediately transferred their allegiance to Jesus. This incident demonstrates the power of John the Baptist's testimony and illustrates how the Gospel spreads through personal witness.

Andrew's Discovery: Andrew, having spent time with Jesus, immediately sought his brother Simon with the announcement: *"We have found the Messias, which is, being interpreted, the Christ"* (**John 1:41**). The joy of discovery compels sharing—those who truly encounter the Lamb of God cannot remain silent about Him.

Philip's Call and Witness: Jesus directly calls Philip, who in turn finds Nathanael with the testimony: *"We have found him, of whom Moses in* *the law, and the prophets, did write, Jesus of Nazareth, the son of Joseph"* (**John 1:45**). Philip's words reveal an understanding that Jesus fulfills Old Testament prophecy, including the sacrificial system with its lamb offerings.

Nathanael's Confession: Despite initial skepticism *"Can there any good thing come out of Nazareth?"*, Nathanael's encounter with Jesus produces immediate faith: *"Rabbi, thou art the Son of God; thou art the King of Israel"* (**John 1:49**). This confession reveals both Christ's divine nature and His royal identity.

Jesus responds to Nathanael's confession with a promise: *"Verily, verily, I say unto you, Hereafter ye shall see heaven open, and the angels of God ascending and descending upon the Son of man"* (**John 1:51**). This allusion to Jacob's ladder (**Genesis 28:12**) presents Christ as the bridge between heaven and earth—a function that would be accomplished through His sacrificial death as the Lamb of God. Jacob, a man distressed due to self-inflicted troubles, rested his weary head on a pillow of rocks. His dreams that night, in his distress, revealed a desire in him to find a way to heaven. Jesus is the way!

THE LAMB REVEALED

THE PERSON OF THE LAMB

John 1 establishes crucial aspects of Christ's Person that make His work as the Lamb of God effective:

True God: His eternal existence, divine nature, and creative power establish His deity. Only God could bear infinite punishment for sin and satisfy God's justice completely.

True Man: His incarnation demonstrates His genuine humanity. Only as man could He serve as our representative and substitute, taking our place under the law's penalty.

Sinless Character: His perfection, witnessed by His being *"full of grace and truth"* (**John 1:14**), qualifies Him as the spotless Lamb required for sacrifice.

Divine-Human Unity: The doctrine of the hypostatic union—two natures in one Person—enables Christ to bridge the infinite gulf between God and man.

THE WORK OF THE LAMB

The chapter also establishes the scope and effectiveness of the Lamb's work:

Universal Provision: He *"taketh away the sin of the world"* (**John 1:29**), indicating that His sacrifice is sufficient for the sins of the world.

Complete Removal: The phrase *"taketh away"* suggests permanent removal rather than temporary covering. Unlike Old Testament sacrifices that were repeated endlessly, Christ's sacrifice is final and complete (**Hebrews 10**).

Spiritual Illumination: As the *"true Light"* (**John 1:9**), He enlightens those who receive Him, giving them spiritual understanding and new birth.

Eternal Life: Those who believe in Him receive *"power to become the sons of God"* (**John 1:12**), experiencing the new birth and adoption into God's family.

THE LAMB IN GLORY

Even while focusing on the Lamb's humiliation and sacrifice, **John 1** anticipates His exaltation:

Future Glory: Christ's promise to show greater things (**John 1:51**) anticipates His resurrection and ascension.

Spirit Baptism: His role as the One who *"baptizeth with the Holy Ghost"* (**John 1:33**) points to His post-resurrection ministry through the Spirit.

Eternal Sonship: His identity as *"the only begotten Son"* (**John 1:14, 18**) establishes His eternal relationship with the Father, which death cannot break.

THE PERSON, THE LAMB

John 1 stands as Scripture's supreme revelation of Christ as both the eternal Word and the sacrificial Lamb. From the heights of His pre-existent glory to the depths of His incarnate humility, the chapter traces His condescension that makes redemption possible. John the Baptist's proclamation, *"Behold the Lamb of God, which taketh away the sin of the world"*, crystallizes centuries of sacrificial typology into one living Person and provides the key to understanding all subsequent revelation about Christ's redemptive work.

The chapter demonstrates that the Lamb of God is simultaneously the eternal Creator who spoke worlds into existence and the temporal sacrifice who yielded His life for sin. He is the Light who lighteth every man and the Lamb who removes the world's darkness through His death. He is the Word who reveals the Father's heart and the sacrifice who satisfies the Father's justice.

For the believer, **John 1** provides both the foundation for faith and the pattern for witness. We proclaim the eternal Son of God who became the Lamb of God for our salvation. Our message, like John's, must be simple and clear: *"Behold the Lamb of God."* In beholding Him, sinners find life; in proclaiming Him, believers fulfill their calling; in worshiping Him, the Church anticipates eternal glory.

The progression from John's Gospel to John's Revelation traces the complete arc of the Lamb's work—from His humble appearance in **John 1** to His glorious reign in **Revelation 22**. He who was proclaimed by John the Baptist will be praised by all creation. He who was received by a few disciples will be recognized by every tongue and tribe. He who took away the sin of the world will reign over the world in righteousness.

"Worthy is the Lamb that was slain, and hath redeemed us to God by his blood out of every kindred, and tongue, and people, and nation" (**Revelation 5:9, 12**). From eternity past to eternity future, from the councils of the Godhead to the cross of Calvary to the throne of glory, Christ remains the same—the eternal Son, the incarnate Word, the sacrificial Lamb, the exalted King. In Him, all the purposes of God find their fulfillment, and all the hopes of humanity find their answer. This is the Lamb of God, proclaimed by John, revealed in Scripture, received by faith, and worshiped throughout eternity.

CHAPTER EIGHT

THE LAMB TAKING AWAY SIN

> **Acts 8:26-40** will demonstrate how the Ethiopian eunuch discovered the Lamb in Isaiah's ancient prophecy, illustrating how New Testament fulfillment illuminates Old Testament prediction and how the Spirit guides sincere seekers to Christ.

PHILIP & THE ETHIOPIAN EUNUCH

UPON A DESOLATE ROAD, where the dust of the Judean desert settles upon the grand ambitions of men, the Spirit of God prepared a stage for one of history's most intimate and momentous revelations. Here, in the divinely orchestrated encounter between Philip the evangelist and the Ethiopian eunuch, the gospel shines not as a new and sudden star, but as the brilliant culmination of a light that had been dawning since the world plunged into sin.

The scarlet thread of redemption, which began with the coats of skins in a lost Eden, runs through this passage with vivid clarity. It is the same thread seen in Abel's more excellent sacrifice, in the ram God provided for Abraham upon Mount Moriah, and in the blood of the Passover lamb that marked the doorposts in a doomed Egypt. For centuries, this truth was taught through the silent, bleeding ministry of animal sacrifices, until the Lamb stepped from the shadows of ritual and was revealed as a Person in the sublime prophecy of **Isaiah 53**. In the narrative of **Acts 8:26—40**, this stream of prophecy, having gathered volume through the ages, breaks forth from the confines of temple rite and ancient scroll into the glorious light of personal salvation.

What a study in godly contrasts the scene presents! A man of *"great authority,"* the treasurer of a queen, returning from a fruitless pilgrimage to worship in Jerusalem, yet inwardly impoverished and perplexed. The Spirit alone could bridge the infinite distance between a Gentile court official—far removed from the temple's hallowed precincts—and the very Lamb proclaimed by John the Baptist and sketched centuries earlier by Isaiah's pen. Here, the great principle of the new dispensation is laid bare: **salvation rests not on human merit or religious pedigree, but entirely on faith in Jesus Christ**. The eunuch's confession, *"I believe that Jesus Christ is the Son of God,"* precedes his baptism, establishing for all time the godly order: **first**, the inward reality of trust in the Lamb; **then**, the outward ordinance of obedience.

Thus, on that lonely highway, the Lamb foreseen by patriarchs and prophets becomes the Saviour trusted by a seeking soul, and the grand tapestry of progressive revelation finds its perfect and personal completion in the joyous testimony of a redeemed man.

DIRECTION IN THE WILDERNESS

"Then the angel of the Lord spake unto Philip, saying, Arise, and go toward the south unto the way that goeth down from Jerusalem unto Gaza, which is desert" (**Acts 8:26**). Here the narrative pauses to display heaven's

whisper: the Holy Spirit supervises every step of this evangelistic advance, knowing the need of both the seeker and the preacher better than they know themselves. It is striking that God's majesty unfolds on a barren desert road rather than in a hallowed synagogue—yet in this unpromising setting His tender pastoral care shines most clearly as He sends His messenger where both need and hearts are open.

Philip's immediate compliance—*"And he arose and went"*—reveals the character of a true servant: swift obedience born of intimate communion with the Spirit. Far from the marble courts of the temple, on that lonely highway between Jerusalem and Gaza, the Lord again demonstrates the dispensational transition: the gospel advancing from Jewish confines to Gentile horizons. Having escaped the persecution that followed Stephen's martyrdom, Philip is sent not back to the safety of the city, but forward into the wilderness, an unlikely venue for redemptive encounter. Thus Scripture weaves its grand scarlet thread into this desert dawn, where a humble evangelist meets a humble official—**and the Lamb of God becomes the treasure of both Jew and Gentile alike.**

THE ETHIOPIAN EUNUCH

This eunuch presents a study in godly contrasts. Scripture describes him as *"a man of Ethiopia, an eunuch of great authority under Candace queen of the Ethiopians, who had the charge of all her treasure, and had come to Jerusalem for to worship"* (**Acts 8:27**). Despite his impressive credentials—high governmental position, obvious education, and considerable wealth—this powerful man remained spiritually unfulfilled.

His pilgrimage to Jerusalem suggests he was either a convert to Judaism or simply an integral God-fearing Gentile attracted to the God of Israel. His possession of Isaiah's prophecy in written format, exceedingly valuable in the ancient world, attests to his earnest spiritual seeking. Yet for all his earthly advantages, when Philip asked, *"Understandest thou what thou readest?"* his humble response revealed human wisdom's limitations: *"How can I, except some man should guide me?"* (**Acts 8:30-31**).

This powerful man's willing admission of need demonstrates true humility. The treasurer of a nation acknowledged that spiritual understanding requires proper guidance from one filled with the Holy Spirit. Such humility remains essential for spiritual growth even today—believers do not mature in faith without the guidance of Spirit-filled teachers willing to expound the Scriptures.

THE LAMB PROPHESIED IN ISAIAH

The portion occupying the Ethiopian's attention was **Isaiah 53:7-8**, describing the suffering servant: *"He was led as a sheep to the slaughter; and like a lamb dumb before his shearer, so opened he not his mouth: In his humiliation his judgment was taken away: and who shall declare his generation? for his life is taken from the earth"* (**Acts 8:32-33**).

This prophetic passage, written approximately seven centuries before Christ's advent, portrays with remarkable precision the Messiah's sacrificial death. The metaphors of sheep and lamb express the innocence, meekness, and patience of Christ in His sufferings. His willingness to be led to slaughter and His silence before accusers demonstrate His voluntary submission to become the sacrifice for sins.

Like a lamb trusting whatever situation it is led into, Christ submitted to those who would strip and slay Him, knowing His purpose was to die for the world's sins. The Ethiopian's honest question—*"of whom speaketh the prophet this? of himself, or of some other man?"*—opened the door for Philip to proclaim the gospel.

PHILIP PREACHES JESUS

When Philip *"opened his mouth, and began at the same scripture, and preached unto him Jesus"* (**Acts 8:35**), he demonstrated the indispensable method of all genuine preaching: **letting Scripture interpret Scripture under the Spirit's guidance**. In that moment, the aged prophecy of **Isaiah 53** ceased to be antique and blazed forth as living, human reality in Jesus Christ. This, for once, demonstrated the scholarly humility required for this task—the readiness to abandon preconceptions and allow the text to speak its singular testimony. Philip did not impose his own notions upon **Isaiah**; rather, he allowed the suffering Servant to unveil Himself until the Ethiopian saw not a distant oracle but the very Person of God's provision.

This procedure mirrors our Lord's post-resurrection encounter on the Emmaus road: *"beginning at Moses and all the prophets, he expounded unto them in all the scriptures the things concerning himself"* (**Luke 24:27**). Imagine the tenderness of such an exposition, where the ancient types and shadows of burnt offerings, Passover lambs, and sin offerings converge upon the Lamb who imbues them with eternal meaning. In each Old Testament utterance, Christ is both the substance and the summation of all that God designed from **Genesis** to **Malachi**.

By unfolding **Isaiah 53** before a foreign dignitary, Philip enacted the grand tapestry of progressive revelation. From Abel's first lamb to Abraham's substitute, from Egypt's passover to Leviticus' sacrificial system, every redemptive milestone was a step toward this moment when the

Lamb slain *"from the foundation of the world"* would stand revealed. Philip led the eunuch beyond academic curiosity into personal faith, demonstrating that true understanding is inseparable from trust in Christ. Thus, the gospel emancipates the heart from abstraction and anchors it in the Person who once bore our griefs and carried our sorrows—Jesus, the Lamb of God, who takes away the sin of the world.

THE CONFESSION OF FAITH

When the Ethiopian requested baptism, Philip stipulated: *"If thou believest with all thine heart, thou mayest."* The eunuch responded with clear confession: *"I believe that Jesus Christ is the Son of God"* (**Acts 8:37**). This confession connects three vital doctrinal concepts.

First, *"Jesus"* is the historical person of Nazareth.

Second, *"Christ"* affirms His messianic office—the term means *"anointed one,"* exactly equivalent to *"Messiah"*.

Third, *"Son of God"* acknowledges Jesus' divine nature and unique relationship with the Father.

This confession demonstrates that early believers understood Jesus not as a prophet or teacher, but as the Messiah, the fulfillment of Old Testament prophecy. The eunuch's confession aligns perfectly with foundational Christian belief that Jesus of Nazareth is the Christ, the Messiah, the Son of God.

SALVATION BY FAITH ALONE

In the wilderness encounter between Philip and the Ethiopian eunuch, the doctrine of salvation by faith alone is cast in the clearest light, stripped of all ritualistic encumbrance. When the Spirit of God opens a man's understanding to the Lamb of God, the soul's immediate response is not one of meritorious action but of simple, unadorned trust.

After Philip *"preached unto him Jesus,"* beginning with the very prophecy of the suffering Lamb from **Isaiah 53**, the eunuch's heart was made ready. Upon seeing water, he did not ask, *"What must I do to be saved?"* for that question had already been answered in the glorious person of the Lamb. Instead, he asked, *"what doth hinder me to be baptized?"*. His question reveals a heart ready to trust in Christ, but perhaps still clouded with the mindset of religious works he had known. There was a hindrance, it was his lack of trust in the Son of God that hindered his water baptism.

Philip's reply establishes the unalterable prerequisite for salvation, which in turn permits the ordinance of water baptism: *"If thou believest with all thine heart, thou mayest"*. Here is the order, from which there can be no deviation: faith is required for salvation, and water baptism is a public presentation of the faith that has already been established. The eunuch's confession—*"I believe that Jesus Christ is the Son of God"*—was the very means of his salvation, for as the scripture affirms, *"if thou shalt confess with thy mouth the Lord Jesus, and shalt believe in thine heart that God hath raised him from the dead, thou shalt be saved"* (**Romans 10:9**). He was saved by calling on the name of the Lord.

The narrative confirms this sequence with beautiful simplicity: following the eunuch's declaration of faith, *"they went down both into the water... and he baptized him"*. This act of immersion, therefore, is not a means of salvation, but a picture of it. It is the public testimony of a soul that has already died with Christ, been buried with Him, and is now risen to walk in newness of life. The joy that followed was not the product of the ordinance, but the overflow of a heart cleansed by the precious blood of Christ. The eunuch *"went on his way rejoicing,"* not because he was wet with the water of baptism, but because he was washed in the blood of the Lamb.

THE SPIRIT'S CONTINUING WORK

The account's conclusion demonstrates the Holy Spirit's ongoing ministry: *"the Spirit of the Lord caught away Philip, that the eunuch saw him no more... But Philip was found at Azotus: and passing through he preached in all the cities, till he came to Caesarea"* (**Acts 8:39-40**). This miraculous transportation reminds us that the Spirit's ways transcend human understanding.

The same Spirit who initiated this appointment with supernatural guidance continued directing Philip's ministry. Meanwhile, the Ethiopian continued *"on his way rejoicing,"* presumably carrying the gospel of Christ back to his homeland. Tradition suggests he became the first to introduce Christianity to Ethiopia, demonstrating how individual conversions advance the gospel globally. The Spirit who orchestrated their meeting separated them, as each had further work to accomplish for the Lord. This reflects Christianity's nature—believers may enjoy brief fellowship before godly assignments separate them for continued service.

THE OLD TESTAMENT FOUNDATION

The Ethiopian's encounter demonstrates the inseparable connection between Old and New Testament revelation. Philip's ability to begin with **Isaiah 53** and proclaim Jesus illustrates how the Old Testament points to Christ. This follows the pattern Jesus Himself established when He *"beginning at Moses and all the prophets, he expounded unto them in all the scriptures the things concerning himself"*.

The fact that an Ethiopian court official—a man of great authority and immense wealth—was in possession of a personal copy of Isaiah's prophecy is, in itself, a testament to God's magnificent orchestration. In an age when such scrolls were exceedingly rare and costly, typically reserved for synagogues, the eunuch's ownership of this precious text highlights not only his high station but also the profound depth of his spiritual hunger. It was no common thing for a traveler on a desert road to be reading from such a treasured manuscript.

Therefore, the Spirit's timing in bringing Philip to this precise moment is all the more striking. God led His servant not to a bustling synagogue, but to a solitary chariot carrying a single, seeking soul who had the rare means to possess the very words of life, yet lacked the understanding that only the Spirit could provide. This was no chance encounter; it was a divine appointment of the highest order. While we have plenty of scripture instructing believers to preach to every creature and sow the seed on every ground, we are also profoundly thankful for such sweetly orchestrated encounters, where God's hand prepares the heart, provides the rare and precious text, and brings His messenger at the perfect time to reveal the Lamb of God.

THE UNIVERSAL SCOPE OF SALVATION

This passage illustrates that the salvation purchased by the Lamb of God demolishes every man-made barrier of ethnicity, wealth, and geography.

The gospel is not a tribal religion or a nationalistic creed; it is a universal invitation to "*whosoever will*".

In the conversion of this Ethiopian official, we see the beautiful fulfillment of Christ's Great Commission beginning to unfold. The geographical and cultural progression is profound: the gospel, having been established in Jerusalem and preached throughout Judea and Samaria, now leaps across the desert sands to reach a dignitary from a distant African nation. What began with Jewish believers in the heart of Israel now reaches a Gentile from what was then considered "*the uttermost part of the earth*," demonstrating with living proof that the Lamb's sacrifice was for the "*sin of the world*".

Through Philip's Spirit-led guidance, the eunuch saw that the suffering servant of **Isaiah** was none other than Jesus Christ, the Son of God. In that moment of belief, every distinction that the world holds dear—his high office, his ethnic background, his physical condition as a eunuch—melted away before the grace of God. The Lamb's blood makes all who trust in it one in Christ.

This very account provides a powerful impetus for the book you now hold. Witnessing how the Spirit of God used the patient unfolding of a single passage of scripture to bring a soul from darkness to light kindles a holy desire to do the same on a larger scale. If one man's explanation of **Isaiah 53** could so radically change a life on a desert road, what might a comprehensive, book-length journey through the entire doctrine of the Lamb accomplish for countless other seeking hearts? It is this hope that fuels the writing of this work—to trace the scarlet thread of redemption from **Genesis** to **Revelation**, so that many, like the Ethiopian, might see Jesus and go on their way rejoicing.

THE LAMB TAKES AWAY SIN

In the encounter on the Gaza road, we witness one of Scripture's most piercing illustrations of the Lamb of God accomplishing His ordained purpose. As John the Baptist's cry, "*Behold the Lamb of God, which taketh away the sin of the world,*" first cut through the air by the Jordan, so here in the dreary futility of the desert, that mighty promise is brought to its intimate and personal consummation. The Spirit-led journey of Philip from the hollow grandeur of Jerusalem's temple courts to a Gentile's solitary chariot is itself a parable of our current dispensation: the gospel, unbound from any single place or people, now travels to the uttermost parts of the earth.

The conversion of the Ethiopian eunuch is a grand confluence, where three realities of redemptive history meet and become one.

First, the **prophecy**, which flowed from Isaiah's pen, ceases to be a distant murmur and becomes a present reality in the Person of Jesus Christ.

Second, the **typology**, which began with the blood of Abel's lamb, swelled with the ram on Moriah, and with the Passover, now finds its full expression in the Lamb slain "*from the foundation of the world*".

Third, God's **universal grace** overflows its banks, demolishing the barriers of ethnicity, social standing, and geography to draw a once-excluded outsider into the very fellowship of God.

The precision of the narrative forbids any notion of coincidence and compels our reverence for the Lord's faithfulness. The costly scroll in the hand of a seeking man, the prepared evangelist arriving at the appointed second, the courageous confession, and the joy that follows—all declare that the ancient promises of God become glorious, experiential certainties the moment a soul trusts in the Lamb. In this wilderness classroom, all the proud scaffolding of human merit—be it ritual, pedigree, or personal effort—is shown to be worthless dust.

Here, the cold abstraction of religious theory gives way to the warm immediacy of a personal Saviour. We behold a man of the highest worldly attainment, returning from the very epicenter of his religious hopes, yet with a soul as barren as the desert around him. The temple had sent him away empty. Yet on a lonely road, the simple unfolding of a single passage of Scripture filled him with a treasure that all the coffers of his queen could not contain. The gospel's power is revealed, not as a system of philosophy to be mastered, but as the Person of Christ to be received—He who *"was wounded for our transgressions"* and *"bruised for our iniquities"* that we might be made whole.

Thus, this account in **Acts 8** marks not only the turning of a page, but the turning of an age. It is the closing of the book of shadows and the opening of the book of substance; the end of prophetic anticipation and the beginning of personal celebration. The Lamb *"without blemish and without spot"* still beckons to seeking souls, inviting all who will to trust in His finished work. Let every reader, then, find encouragement in this sacred history. Your own desert of confusion or spiritual longing may be the very place God has appointed for your own encounter. And having found the Lamb, may you, like that court official of old, go on your way rejoicing—a living testimony that Jesus Christ, the Lamb of God, does indeed take away the sin of the world.

CHAPTER NINE

WITHOUT SPOT & WITHOUT BLEMISH

1 Peter 1:18-21 serves as our theological foundation, establishing that redemption requires a price beyond human ability to pay—the precious blood of Christ as the spotless Lamb foreordained before the foundation of the world.

THE CORNERSTONE OF TRUTH

IN THE SACRED PASSAGE that stands as the cornerstone of this entire study, the Apostle Peter unfurls the scarlet tapestry of our redemption with apostolic authority. He vividly contrasts the corruptible impotence of silver and gold with *"the precious blood of Christ, as of a lamb without blemish and without spot."* Here, the faint echoes of every Old Testament sacrifice—every lamb slain from Abel onward—swell into a final, thunderous declaration. Peter, an eyewitness to the Lamb's majesty, proclaims the perfect offering: a sacrifice foreordained before the foundation of the world, and one sufficient not only to redeem our souls, but to establish our faith and hope in God forever.

THE CALL TO HOLY LIVING

Before the Apostle Peter unfurls the glorious banner of our redemption, he first establishes the practical conduct that must flow from it. His solemn *"Wherefore"* in **verse 13** is a hinge, swinging from the certainty of our inheritance to the consecration of our lives. The logic is inescapable: because our hope is so certain, our holiness must be our chief aim.

Peter issues a threefold command for the redeemed mind: **gird it up** with truth, stripping away worldly distractions that would cause us to stumble; keep it **sober** with spiritual vigilance, weighing all things by God's unchanging word; and fix its **hope** steadfastly on the grace that will be brought to us at Christ's return.

This mindset gives birth to a transformed life. As *"obedient children,"* we are no longer to be fashioned by the ignorant lusts of our past but by the holy character of the God who saved us. The command, *"Be ye holy; for I am holy,"* is not a new suggestion but an eternal standard, echoing from the pages of **Leviticus**. It is the family likeness that should mark every child of God. The awesome price of our redemption, which Peter is about to declare, is the very power that makes this holy conversation possible.

THE PRECIOUS BLOOD OF THE PERFECT LAMB

Here, the Apostle Peter brings us into the very holy of holies of redemptive truth. With the tenderness of a pastor and the precision of an apostle, he lays bare the heart of the gospel: *"Forasmuch as ye know that ye were not redeemed with corruptible things, as silver and gold, from your vain conversation received by tradition from your fathers; But with the precious blood of Christ, as of a lamb without blemish and without spot"* (**1 Peter 1:18–19**).

Peter begins by shattering the foundations of all human religion and philosophy. He forces us to confront what *cannot* redeem the soul. **Silver and gold,** the universal measure of earthly value, are dismissed as *"corruptible things"*. They are the currency of a dying world, powerless to purchase a pardon from a holy God or to cleanse a single stain from a guilty conscience. They are costly, but they cannot save.

Worse still is the *"vain conversation received by tradition from your fathers"*. This is the spiritual bankruptcy we inherit, the empty and futile way of life passed down from Adam through every generation. It is a legacy of ignorance and bondage, a life shaped by sinful lusts and temporal vanities, from which no man can free himself.

Against this backdrop of utter human insolvency, Peter lifts up the price. What all the treasuries of earth and all the traditions of men cannot accomplish, the *"precious blood of Christ"* achieves with finality and perfection. The word *"precious"* denotes not only something of high cost, but something of infinite, intrinsic, and beloved worth.

This blood belongs to the one perfect *"lamb without blemish and without spot"*. The language is a direct echo of the Levitical code, recalling the unceasing inspection of sacrificial animals. Any creature with a mark or wound was an insult to the holiness of God. Christ, our Lamb, endured the severest scrutiny of both God and man, and was found perfect.

He was *"without blemish,"* speaking of His inherent, internal perfection. He possessed no fallen nature, no inherited corruption, no inward inclination toward sin that would disqualify Him as our substitute.

He was *"without spot,"* declaring His external, behavioral perfection. Throughout His entire life, from the manger to the cross, no stain of personal transgression ever marred His perfect obedience to the Father.

This twofold purity—perfect in His nature and perfect in His conduct—is what qualified Him to be the final and complete sacrifice for sin. The blood of bulls and goats could only cover sin temporarily, pointing forward with bleeding figures to the reality to come. But the precious blood of this Lamb, the sinless Son of God, does not simply cover—it cleanses, it redeems, and it reconciles forever all who will trust in Him.

THE ETERNAL PLAN OF REDEMPTION

Here, the Apostle Peter lifts our gaze from the dust of time to the unclouded brilliance of eternity, revealing that the sacrifice of Christ was no emergency measure or afterthought. It was, rather, the fulfillment of God's determinate counsel, the master stroke of a plan conceived by the Lord's foreknowledge (**Acts 2:23**).

"Who verily was foreordained before the foundation of the world, but was manifest in these last times for you, Who by him do believe in God, that raised him up from the dead, and gave him glory; that your faith and hope might be in God" (**1 Peter 1:20–21**).

The word *"foreordained"* speaks of God's settled, determined counsel. In the silent councils of the Godhead, before the world was ever spoken into being, the Son was appointed to be the Lamb. The incarnation, the sinless life, the agonies of the cross, and the triumph of the resurrection were not a reaction to the Fall of man, but the eternally planned *remedy* for it.

This profound truth accomplishes three things for the believing heart:

It reveals the depth of God's love. He did not wait for our cry of distress; He provided the remedy before we were even aware of our need.

It proves the immutability of God's purpose. No rebellion of man or rage of devils could ever frustrate the plan that was set in eternity.

It guarantees the sufficiency of Christ's sacrifice. The God who designed the plan of redemption ensured its absolute perfection and certain success.

Yet what was planned in eternity had to be performed in history. Christ *"was manifest in these last times for you"*. At the precise moment ordained by the Father, *"when the fulness of the time was come,"* the eternal Word became flesh and dwelt among us. He lived, He died for our sins, and He rose again, all according to the scriptures.

For Peter, the resurrection is the triumphant vindication of the entire plan. God *"raised him up from the dead, and gave him glory,"* a public declaration to all creation that the sacrifice of the Lamb was accepted, the debt of sin was paid in full, and death itself was vanquished. It is upon this unshakable, historical fact that our souls find their anchor. Because Christ is risen, our redemption is not a hopeful theory but a glorious reality. And it is for this reason, Peter concludes, that our *"faith and hope might be in God"*—the God who planned, the God who provided, and the God who, in raising His Son, guaranteed the eternal security of all who trust in Him.

BORN AGAIN THROUGH THE INCORRUPTIBLE WORD

Peter connects our redemption through Christ's blood to our regeneration through God's word: *"Being born again, not of corruptible seed, but of incorruptible, by the word of God, which liveth and abideth for ever"* (**1 Peter 1:23**).

Physical birth occurs through *"corruptible seed"*—the natural process of human generation that produces mortal life subject to decay and death. But spiritual birth occurs through *"incorruptible seed"*—the eternal, living word of God that produces eternal life. This word (**scripture**) is described as both *"living"* (**possessing inherent life**) and *"abiding"* (**permanent and unchanging**).

The blood of Christ secures our **redemption**—our full deliverance and ransom from the penalty and power of sin—so that we stand justified before God. His precious blood answers for our guilt and purchases our release (**1 Peter 1:18–19**). The word of God, by contrast, effects our **regeneration**—the new birth wrought by the Holy Spirit—so that we pass from death unto life (**James 1:18; 1 Peter 1:23**). As the incorruptible seed, the word brings forth spiritual life in the believer. Thus, the Lamb's blood procures our legal standing, and the living word imparts our spiritual transformation, both essential to complete salvation

This truth emphasizes the absolute necessity of scripture in God's redemptive work. While many claim spiritual experiences apart from God's written revelation, **Peter** makes clear that the new birth occurs specifically *"by the word of God."* Faith comes by hearing, and hearing by the word of God (**Romans 10:17**). Apart from scripture, there can be no genuine spiritual birth.

THE TRANSFORMING POWER OF REDEMPTION

The apostle demonstrates how redemption through the Lamb's blood produces practical transformation: *"Seeing ye have purified your souls in obeying the truth through the Spirit unto unfeigned love of the brethren, see that ye love one another with a pure heart fervently"* (**1 Peter 1:22**).

The phrase *"purified your souls in obeying the truth"* refers to the cleansing that occurs when we respond in faith to the gospel. *"Obeying the truth"* means believing and receiving the preaching of salvation through Christ's blood—what Paul calls *"the obedience of faith"* (**Romans 1:5**). This spiritual purification enables *"unfeigned love of the brethren"*—genuine, sincere affection for fellow believers.

The command to *"love one another with a pure heart fervently"* follows naturally from our redemption. Because we have been cleansed by the Lamb's blood, we now possess the capacity for pure love. This love springs from a heart that has been made pure through Christ's sacrifice, and it expresses itself in fervent devotion to our brothers and sisters in Christ.

Notice the progression: redemption through Christ's blood → purification of the soul → capacity for genuine love → the command to exercise that love fervently. The doctrine of the Lamb is never limited to academic understanding—it produces practical holiness in those who truly comprehend its meaning.

THE ETERNAL WORD VERSUS THE TEMPORAL WORLD

Peter concludes this section by contrasting the permanence of God's word with the transience of earthly glory: *"For all flesh is as grass, and all the glory of man as the flower of grass. The grass withereth, and the flower thereof falleth away: But the word of the Lord endureth for ever. And this is the word which by the gospel is preached unto you"* (**1 Peter 1:24-25**).

Quoting from **Isaiah 40:6-8**, Peter reminds us that human life and achievement are temporary. *"All flesh is as grass"*—what appears strong and permanent proves fragile and fleeting. *"All the glory of man"*—earthly achievements, honors, and accomplishments—are like flowers that bloom briefly and then fade away.

But *"the word of the Lord endureth for ever."* The same word that accomplishes our regeneration also provides permanent security for our faith. While everything earthly passes away, God's promises remain firm, His truth stands unchanged, and His redemptive work through the Lamb continues to save souls across the generations.

The final phrase is crucial: *"And this is the word which by the gospel is preached unto you."* The eternal, abiding word of God has been proclaimed to us in the gospel. This gospel centers on Christ as the Lamb of God who takes away the sin of the world. Because this word is eternal, the salvation it promises is eternal. Because this word is incorruptible, the life it imparts is incorruptible.

THE UNITY OF SCRIPTURE IN THE LAMB

1 Peter 1:13-24 demonstrates the remarkable unity of scripture in its presentation of the Lamb of God. Peter's language deliberately echoes Old Testament imagery and requirements, showing how Christ fulfills every type and shadow presented in earlier revelation.

The requirement that sacrificial animals be *"without blemish and without spot"* finds its perfect fulfillment in Christ, the spotless Lamb. The prophetic description of the suffering servant in **Isaiah 53** reaches its culmination in Peter's presentation of Christ's redemptive work. The eternal purposes of God, hinted at throughout Old Testament scripture, are revealed clearly in the apostle's teaching about Christ being *"foreordained before the foundation of the world"*.

This unity could never have been achieved by human coordination across the centuries. It stands as powerful evidence for the inspiration of scripture and the supernatural orchestration of God's redemptive plan. The same Spirit who moved upon the Old Testament writers to record types and shadows also inspired the New Testament authors to reveal their fulfillment in Christ.

THE LAMB'S BLOOD AND ASSURANCE

The doctrine of the Lamb provides unshakeable assurance to every believer. Peter's emphasis on the *"precious blood of Christ"* as our redemption price guarantees the eternal security of all who trust in Him. If God paid such an infinite price for our salvation—the blood of His own Son—He will certainly preserve those whom He has purchased.

Moreover, Christ's resurrection and glorification, which Peter emphasizes, demonstrate that the Father accepted His sacrifice and that our redemption is complete. We are not hoping that our salvation will be accomplished someday; we can rejoice that it has been accomplished already through the Lamb's finished work.

The incorruptible nature of our new birth, accomplished through the eternal word of God, provides additional assurance. Because we have been *"born again, not of corruptible seed, but of incorruptible,"* our spiritual life can never decay or die. The same word that created spiritual life within us continues to sustain and preserve that life throughout our earthly pilgrimage.

LOOKING FORWARD TO GLORY

Peter's presentation of the Lamb concludes with forward-looking hope. The *"grace that is to be brought unto you at the revelation of Jesus Christ"* speaks of the complete salvation that awaits us when our Lord returns in glory.

The Lamb who was slain will return as the Lion of the tribe of Judah. The One who suffered humiliation will appear in magnificent glory. The Savior who bore our sins will come to reign in righteousness. For those who have been redeemed by His precious blood, that future appearing is not a day of dread but **the blessed hope that motivates present holiness** and sustains current faith.

Until that glorious day, we live as *"strangers and pilgrims"* in this world, our hearts set on things above where Christ sits at the right hand of God. The doctrine of the Lamb reminds us that our citizenship is in heaven, our inheritance is incorruptible, and our future is secure in the hands of Him who loves us and gave Himself for us.

THE LAMB'S COMPLETE WORK

In this passage from his first epistle, the Apostle Peter, guided by the Holy Ghost, has taken us again from the shadows of the Old Testament into the blazing light of its New Testament fulfillment. He has shown us the grand, sweeping panorama of redemption, a work so vast it was planned in eternity, and so powerful it secures our hope for eternity. Here, in these few verses, we find the entire doctrine of the Lamb in its breathtaking completeness.

We see His **eternal election**, for this Lamb was *"foreordained before the foundation of the world,"* the centerpiece of God's purpose. We see His **perfect qualification** as a lamb *"without blemish and without spot,"* the only sacrifice whose inherent and behavioral purity could satisfy the demands of a holy God. We see His **complete accomplishment** through the shedding of His *"precious blood,"* a currency of infinite value that achieved what all the silver and gold on earth never could. We see His **divine vindication**, for God *"raised him up from the dead, and gave him glory,"* publicly stamping the sacrifice with His seal of absolute approval and acceptance. Finally, we see His **transforming application**, as this redemption purifies our souls, gives us a living hope, and becomes the very foundation upon which our faith rests.

The progression of God's revelation is now perfected. What began with the faint whisper of a blood sacrifice in **Genesis** has crescendoed into this thunderous declaration of victory.

The **type** has given way to the **Antitype**. Every lamb that bled on a patriarchal altar was but a dim picture; Christ is the glorious reality.

Prophecy has dissolved into **performance**. The suffering Servant whom **Isaiah** saw in vision has now been *"manifest in these last times for you"*.

Ceremony has been fulfilled in **Christ**. The shadows of the Mosaic law have fled before the substance of the Son of God, who is the end of the law for righteousness to every one that believeth.

Yet, most remarkably, this doctrine is no museum piece of historical theology. It is a living, breathing power that invades and transforms our present experience. Because we have been redeemed by this Lamb, we are now called to live as the redeemed. The same perfection that qualified Christ to be our sacrifice now becomes the standard and power for our sanctification. We are summoned to a holy conversation, not as a means to earn salvation, but as the inevitable and joyful *fruit* of having received it so freely. The blood that purchased our pardon also provides the power for our purity.

And what shall be our response to such a salvation? Our hearts can do nothing else but join the unceasing anthem of the heavens, ascribing all worth to the one who is worthy: "*Worthy is the Lamb that was slain to receive power, and riches, and wisdom, and strength, and honour, and glory, and blessing*". The Lamb of God, who took away the sin of the world, is worthy of our highest praise, our deepest love, and our most devoted service.

Therefore, the doctrine of the Lamb as revealed by Peter does not leave us in the realm of abstract thought; it issues a threefold call to action. It calls us to **live worthy** of such a great salvation, to **walk worthy** of such a glorious Savior, and to **hope confidently** in such a certain future. Until that day when faith shall give way to sight, may our lives be a continual testimony to the world of the transforming power of His precious blood and the surpassing worth of His perfect sacrifice.

CHAPTER TEN

THE LAMB, THE WORTHY REDEEMER

Revelation 5 will present the glorified Lamb upon His eternal throne, worthy to open the sealed book and execute judgment because He was slain—showing how past suffering qualifies for future exaltation.

THE WORTHY REDEEMER

REVELATION 5:6 *And I beheld, and, lo, in the midst of the throne and of the four beasts, and in the midst of the elders, stood a Lamb as it had been slain, having seven horns and seven eyes, which are the seven Spirits of God sent forth into all the earth.*

Here, in the very heart of John's Spirit-guided writings, stands the culmination of all redemptive history—the Lamb of God, slain yet living, worthy to execute the final purposes of the Almighty. Following the magnificent throne room scene of **chapter 4**, where the Lord is worshipped in His unapproachable glory, a dramatic and solemn tension unfolds. John sees in the Lord's right hand a book, sealed with seven seals, containing the unfolding of God's final redemptive plan for His creation.

A mighty angel issues a challenge that echoes through all existence: *"Who is worthy to open the book, and to loose the seals thereof?"* (**Revelation 5:2**). A profound silence follows. The search is universal and exhaustive—no man in heaven, nor in earth, neither under the earth, is able to open the book. The destiny of creation seemingly hangs in the balance, and John, understanding the devastating implications, *"wept much, because no man was found worthy"* (**Revelation 5:4**).

It is in this moment of utter human and creaturely inadequacy that hope appears. An elder comforts him, saying, *"Weep not: behold, the Lion of the tribe of Juda, the Root of David, hath prevailed to open the book, and to loose the seven seals thereof"* (**Revelation 5:5**). These are Messianic titles of the highest order, promising a King of unconquerable strength and righteous authority. Yet, when John turns to see this mighty Lion, **he beholds a Lamb**, standing *"as it had been slain"*.

This is the central paradox of the Gospel, displayed in heaven's throne room: **the conquering Lion is the sacrificial Lamb**. His power does not come from overwhelming force, but from His atoning death. His victory was achieved not by destroying His enemies, but by bearing their sins in His own body on the tree. The very marks of His slaughter remain on His glorified body, an eternal testimony that His right to rule was purchased with His own blood.

The Lamb's appearance is rich with symbolism:

Seven Horns: In scripture, horns represent power and authority. Seven horns signify **perfect and complete power**. Though He submitted to death, the Lamb holds all authority.

Seven Eyes: These represent **perfect knowledge and wisdom**. Nothing in all creation is hidden from His sight.

The Seven Spirits of God: This likely refers to the **fullness of the Holy Spirit**, as prophesied in **Isaiah 11:2**. The Lamb is the one who sends forth the Spirit's perfect, seven-fold ministry into all the earth.

His worthiness is explicitly tied to His sacrifice. The heavenly host declares, *"Thou art worthy to take the book, and to open the seals thereof: **for thou wast slain, and hast redeemed us to God by thy blood** out of every kindred, and tongue, and people, and nation"* (**Revelation 5:9**). His authority flows directly from His atoning work.

It is here we must take care to rightly divide the word of truth. The sealed book, containing the judgments and restoration of the earth, pertains to God's dispensational program for Israel and the nations. The church, having already been caught up to meet the Lord in the air, is represented by the twenty-four elders, observing these events from heaven.

This glorious vision leaves no room for human pride or self-sufficiency. No one was found worthy. Therefore, let every reader abandon all hope in his own merit and look to the only one who can unseal the book. The Lamb of God, Jesus Christ, who was slain for our sins, is alone worthy of our trust, our worship, and our eternal praise. In Him, and in Him alone, is the power to save, the wisdom to guide, and the authority to bring all of God's holy purposes to their triumphant conclusion.

THE MYSTERY OF THE SEALED BOOK

The scene opens with John's attention drawn to *"a book written within and on the backside, sealed with seven seals"* in the right hand of Him that sat upon the throne. This scroll, with writing on both sides, indicates its contents were comprehensive and complete—every available space contained vital information. The sealing with seven seals suggests perfect security; the number seven throughout scripture represents completeness and perfection. No portion of its contents could be accessed until one with proper authority broke those seals.

When a strong angel issues the challenge with a loud voice, "*Who is worthy to open the book, and to loose the seals thereof?*" the resulting silence creates an unbearable tension. The search extends through all creation—"*no man in heaven, nor in earth, neither under the earth, was able to open the book, neither to look thereon*"—yet none is found worthy. This comprehensive search emphasizes the absolute uniqueness of Christ's worthiness and the impossibility of any created being fulfilling this role.

The depth of John's emotional response—he "*wept much*"—indicates the crucial importance of this sealed document. John's weeping was not only sentimental but was a prophetic grief over the implications: if no one could open this book, then all of creation would remain under its present bondage, and God's redemptive purposes would be thwarted.

THE NATURE OF THE SCROLL

This sealed book has been interpreted variously throughout church history. Some view it as representing the **title deed to the earth**, the document that grants its holder the right to possess and rule the kingdoms of the world. This interpretation finds biblical support in the legal customs of ancient Israel, particularly in **Jeremiah 32**. In that chapter, the prophet **Jeremiah** is commanded by God to purchase a field, even as the Babylonian army is about to conquer the land. He seals the deed of purchase and has it stored in an earthen vessel for preservation, as a testimony that God would one day restore the land to its rightful owners. In the same way, this heavenly scroll can be seen as God's claim upon His creation, awaiting the worthy redeemer to take possession.

While it is true that the "*kingdoms of this world*" were offered to Christ by Satan (**Matthew 4:8–11**), this was a temptation to seize power illegitimately, bypassing the cross. Satan is the "*god of this world*" (**2 Corinthians 4:4**) only by usurpation, not by right. Adam forfeited mankind's dominion, and Christ, as the "*last Adam,*" must redeem it through His perfect obedience and sacrificial death. The scroll in God's hand is not a lost title deed, but one held in security until the Kinsman-Redeemer reclaims it.

Other interpretations suggest the book contains God's comprehensive **redemptive program**, which is enacted through the judgments that follow the breaking of the seals. These views are not mutually exclusive. The scroll can be both the title deed to creation and the blueprint for its redemption, outlining the judgments necessary to evict the usurper and establish Christ's righteous kingdom. What remains certain is that this book contains the final purposes of God for the consummation of all things, and only One with absolute, earned worthiness could unseal its contents and execute its decrees.

THE LION WHO IS A LAMB

The dramatic resolution to John's weeping comes through an elder's declaration: "*Weep not: behold, the Lion of the tribe of Judah, the Root of David, hath prevailed to open the book, and to loose the seven seals thereof*" (**Revelation 5:5**). These titles connect Christ directly to the

Messianic prophecies of the Old Testament, identifying Him as the fulfillment of God's covenant promises to Israel. The title **Lion of the tribe of Judah** hearkens back to Jacob's prophecy in **Genesis 49:9–10**, designating the royal, ruling authority of the Messiah. The **Root of David** recalls Isaiah's promise of a **righteous Branch** from the stump of Jesse (**Isaiah 11:1**), signifying both Davidic kingship and divine origin. Together, they evoke an image of immense strength, majesty, and conquering power—the victorious Messiah who would rule with unquestionable authority.

Yet when John turns to behold this mighty Lion, he sees instead "*a Lamb as it had been slain*" (**Revelation 5:6**). This striking contrast constitutes scripture's most profound paradox: the conquering one is also the sacrificed one; **the Lion is the Lamb.** The text deliberately juxtaposes these seemingly contradictory images to reveal the essential mystery of redemption—that God's greatest power is revealed not in coercive force, but in sacrificial love.

The Lamb appears "*as it had been slain,*" indicating that the marks of His sacrificial death remain visible even in His glorified state. When believers see their Savior in glory, they will behold the evidence of His suffering on their behalf. This vision fulfills the prophecy of **Zechariah**, who foretold a day **when Israel would look upon Him whom they pierced and mourn (Zechariah 12:10).** The question posed in **Zechariah 13:6**, "*What are these wounds in thine hands?*" is answered with the solemn words, "*Those with which I was wounded in the house of my friends,*" pointing to the historical reality of His rejection and crucifixion.

This paradoxical nature of Christ as both Lion and Lamb reveals the central mystery of redemption. Christ was a spotless lamb who took on death without iniquity, yet as a lion He slew death and took the victory. The text identifies Jesus as **the Lamb that was slain**, highlighting that His conquering power derives not from military might or political dominance, but from His sacrificial death. His victory was accomplished not by destroying His enemies but by offering Himself as the perfect sacrifice for their sins.

This imagery fundamentally transforms our understanding of true power. Godly strength is displayed most perfectly through sacrifice and willing submission to the Father's will. It is the foundation of the Christian life: the way up is down, true greatness comes through service, and God's ultimate victory over evil was secured through the Lamb's willing sacrifice for the redemption of souls.

THE WORTHINESS OF THE LAMB

The central question driving the narrative of **Revelation 5** is: "*Who is worthy to open the book, and to loose the seals thereof?*". This question of worthiness pervades the entire chapter, appearing in the angel's proclamation, the subsequent universal silence, and the eventual celebration that erupts when the worthy one is found. The worthiness of the Lamb stems directly from His sacrificial death, as the heavenly chorus declares: "*Thou art worthy to take the book, and to open the seals thereof: for thou wast slain, and hast redeemed us to God by thy blood out of every kindred, and tongue, and people, and nation*" (**Revelation 5:9**).

His worthiness is not based on inherent power or position alone, though He certainly possesses both as the eternal Son of God, but is explicitly tied to His **redemptive work**. This establishes the profound biblical principle that true authority flows from sacrifice and service rather than from self-assertion or conquest. As the Apostle Paul wrote in **Philippians 2:8-9**, it was *because* Christ "*humbled himself, and became obedient unto death, even the death of the cross,*" that "*God also hath highly exalted him, and given him a name which is above every name.*" His exaltation is the Father's response to His humiliation.

The Lamb's worthiness is further established through His perfect fulfillment of the requirements for a **kinsman-redeemer**. Under Old Testament law, a kinsman-redeemer had to meet several qualifications: he needed to be a near kinsman, be willing to redeem, and be able to pay the redemption price.

Christ fulfilled these requirements perfectly:

He became our Kinsman: By taking on human flesh, He became related to those He came to redeem (**Hebrews 2:14–17**).

He was willing to redeem: He willingly offered Himself as our sacrifice, demonstrating His great love for us (**John 10:15, Revelation 1:5**).

He was able to pay the price: Possessing the infinite value of a sinless life, His precious blood was the only currency sufficient to purchase our redemption (**1 Peter 1:18–19**).

This connection to the concept of the kinsman-redeemer confirms that the Lamb's worthiness to open the scroll is directly related to His completed work of purchasing mankind and the earth itself through His blood. His death was not a tragic martyrdom but the intentional payment of the full price required to reclaim all that had been lost through Adam's fall.

The word "*prevailed*" used in **verse 5** signifies a victory won through struggle. Christ accomplished something that qualified Him for this unique role—He overcame the world, sin, death, and Satan through His sacrificial death and glorious resurrection. In essence, His death was not a defeat but a triumphant accomplishment, the *"decease which he should accomplish at Jerusalem"* (**Luke 9:31**).

THE ATTRIBUTES OF THE SLAIN LAMB

John's vision presents the Lamb with distinctive features that illuminate His nature and authority. He describes the Lamb as having "*seven horns and seven eyes, which are the seven Spirits of God sent forth into all the earth*" (**Revelation 5:6**). These attributes carry profound meaning, reinforcing Christ's absolute authority despite His appearance as a slain sacrifice.

The Seven Horns: the Lamb's **perfect power and strength**. Throughout scripture, horns consistently represent power, might, and authority—the ability to enforce one's will and overcome all opposition. That the Lamb possesses seven horns—the number of completeness and perfection—indicates He has absolute power, lacking nothing required to accomplish His purposes. Though He voluntarily submitted to the weakness of death, He retains all power in heaven and in earth (**Matthew 28:18**). In **Revelation 11**, he will begin to take up and exercise that great power.

The Seven Eyes: explicitly identified as "*the seven Spirits of God sent forth into all the earth,*" represent His **perfect knowledge and wisdom**. Nothing escapes His attention; He sees and knows what He wills. This imagery connects directly to the seven-fold description of the Holy

Spirit who would rest upon the Messiah, as prophesied in **Isaiah 11:2**: the Spirit of the LORD, the spirit of wisdom, understanding, counsel, might, knowledge, and of the fear of the LORD. This shows that the Lamb operates with the fullness of godly wisdom and discernment.

Thus, even while bearing the marks of slaughter, the Lamb possesses both perfect power (*seven horns*) and perfect knowledge (*seven eyes*). This is a vivid portrayal of how Christ's apparent weakness in death concealed His ultimate authority and ability. The number seven in each case emphasizes the **completeness and perfection** of these attributes, assuring the believer that the One who was slain will take absolute control when He is ready.

UNIVERSAL WORSHIP OF THE LAMB

The latter portion of **Revelation 5** depicts an expanding circle of worship directed toward the Lamb. This worship begins with the four living creatures and the twenty-four elders, extends to a number of angels that is ten thousand times ten thousand, and thousands of thousands, and finally encompasses *"every creature which is in heaven, and on the earth, and under the earth"* (**Revelation 5:11, 13**). The universal scope of this worship underscores the significance of the Lamb's redemptive work and establishes His worthiness to receive praise equal to that given to God the Father.

The **twenty-four elders** are best understood as representing the raptured church in its glorified state, having been brought to heaven before the tribulation begins.

Their **white robes** symbolize the imputed righteousness of Christ.

Their **golden crowns** represent the rewards given for faithful service.

Their position on **thrones** indicates their promised future reign with Christ.

That they hold *"harps and golden vials full of odours, which are the prayers of the saints"* (**Revelation 5:8**) shows their priestly function, presenting the worship and petitions of God's people before His throne.

The content of this worship further illuminates the Lamb's worthiness. The heavenly beings declare Him worthy to receive *"power, and riches, and wisdom, and strength, and honour, and glory, and blessing"* (**Revelation 5:12**). This sevenfold ascription of praise encompasses every possible domain of authority and excellence. Their song specifically connects this worthiness to His redemptive sacrifice: *"for thou wast slain, and hast redeemed us to God by thy blood"*.

The praise continues with the recognition that the Lamb has made those He redeemed *"kings and priests unto our God: and we shall reign on the earth"* (**Revelation 5:10**). This indicates that His sacrifice not only purchases forgiveness but also establishes a new, elevated status and purpose for the redeemed. The saints of the church age receive privileges unique to this dispensation—we are made members of His body, the bride of Christ, and co-heirs with Him in His coming kingdom.

The worship culminates with all creation joining in a unified chorus, pronouncing equal blessing upon *"him that sitteth upon the throne, and unto the Lamb for ever and ever"* (**Revelation 5:13**). This powerful affirmation places the Lamb on the same level of adoration as God the Father, providing undeniable scriptural proof of His absolute deity and His equal worthiness to receive worship.

THE LAMB'S REDEMPTIVE PURPOSE

The significance of the Lamb imagery in **Revelation 5** connects directly to Christ's redemptive work as foretold throughout scripture. John the Baptist had previously identified Jesus as *"the Lamb of God, which taketh away the sin of the world"* (**John 1:29**), and **Isaiah 53** prophesied the suffering Savior who was led like a lamb to the slaughter. The Lamb in **Revelation** represents the glorious fulfillment of all sacrificial lambs in the Old Testament system—He is the perfect and final sacrifice that actually accomplishes what the types and shadows could only symbolize.

His blood provides genuine and permanent cleansing from sin, not the symbolic and temporary purification offered by animal sacrifices. Under the Law, *"it is not possible that the blood of bulls and of goats should take away sins"* (**Hebrews 10:4**). Those sacrifices served as a constant reminder of sin, not its final removal. But Christ, *"by his own blood... obtained eternal redemption for us"* (**Hebrews 9:12**).

The Lamb's worthiness stems specifically from His sacrificial death that ransomed a people for God *"out of every kindred, and tongue, and people, and nation"* (**Revelation 5:9**). This universal scope of redemption highlights that Christ's sacrifice transcends all human barriers—national, ethnic, linguistic, and cultural. The gospel is for *"whosoever will,"* regardless of background or station in life.

The Lamb's blood accomplishes both forgiveness and transformation, making the redeemed *"kings and priests"* who *"shall reign on the earth"* (**Revelation 5:10**). This indicates that redemption includes not only rescue from the penalty of judgment but also elevation to a royal and priestly status—a complete reversal of man's fallen condition. What was lost in Adam, and more, is regained in Christ.

The paradoxical nature of this redemption—that victory comes through apparent defeat, that life springs from death, and that weakness overcomes strength—stands at the heart of the gospel message and finds its most perfect expression in the image of the slain yet glorified Lamb.

THE VICTORY OF THE SACRIFICIAL LAMB

Revelation 5 presents a magnificent vision that unites sacrifice with triumph, suffering with victory, and apparent defeat with ultimate conquest. The Lamb who was slain yet lives forever embodies the central paradox of redemption: that God's power is made perfect in weakness, that Christ conquered by voluntary submission, that He gained life for others by surrendering His own.

This imagery redefines our understanding of true power, showing that authority based on love and self-sacrifice stands infinitely superior to that based on coercion or domination. The world's way is to grasp for power and position, but Christ's way is to humble oneself in service to others. As He taught His disciples, *"whosoever will be great among you, let him be your minister; and whosoever will be chief among you, let him be your servant"* (**Matthew 20:26-27**).

The Lamb of God in **Revelation 5** is worthy to unveil and execute God's purposes for the culmination of history. This worthiness stems from His willing sacrifice that purchased souls from every nation. The universal worship He receives confirms His status as God and establishes the foundation for the judgments and events that will unfold in subsequent chapters.

Throughout the remainder of **Revelation**, the title *"Lamb"* becomes the predominant designation for Christ, appearing twenty-eight times and serving as the lens through which all other aspects of His character and work are understood. Whether opening seals of judgment, receiving the worship of the redeemed, or reigning in the New Jerusalem, He is consistently presented as *"the Lamb."*

THE ETERNAL PERSPECTIVE

In this paradox of the Lamb who conquers, we find the essence of Christian faith: that the way up is down, that true greatness comes through service, and that God's ultimate victory over evil comes through sacrificing Himself for the redemption of souls. This truth should transform how believers approach authority, leadership, and relationships with others.

The scene in **Revelation 5** also provides great comfort during trials and tribulations. While evil seems to prosper and injustice appears to prevail, we know that the Lamb has already overcome and will ultimately execute perfect justice. The sealed book will be opened, its contents will be revealed, and all of God's purposes will be accomplished through the worthy Lamb.

For those who have trusted in the Lamb's sacrificial death, this passage assures us of our eternal security and future glory. We are part of that redeemed company from *"every kindred, and tongue, and people, and nation"* who will cast our crowns before His throne and sing the new song of redemption. What a day that will be when we see the Lamb in all His glory and join the universal chorus of praise!

Until that glorious day arrives, we live as those who know the end of the story. Evil will not ultimately triumph, death will not have the final word, and Satan's rebellion will be completely defeated. The Lamb who was slain has prevailed, and in Him we have both present peace and future hope. He alone is worthy of our worship, our service, and our complete devotion.

SACRIFICE, REDEMPTION, WORTHINESS

As we conclude this study of the Lamb in **Revelation 5**, we are compelled to worship. Here we see the culmination of all scripture's teaching about sacrifice, redemption, and the worthiness of Christ. From Abel's lamb to the Passover lamb, from the Day of Atonement offerings to **Isaiah's** suffering servant, all find their fulfillment in the Lamb who stands in the midst of the throne.

The doctrine of the Lamb of God reaches its magnificent climax in this passage, showing us that Jesus Christ—the Lion of Judah and the Root of David, the slain yet living Lamb—is uniquely qualified and eternally worthy to accomplish all of God's redemptive purposes. His worthiness rests not upon power or position, but upon His perfect sacrifice that redeemed a people for God from every nation under heaven.

May this glorious vision of the worthy Lamb inflame our hearts with love for Him who loved us and gave Himself for us. May it motivate us to live worthy of such a salvation, to serve worthy of such a Savior, and to hope confidently in such a future. And may it prepare us for that day when we shall see Him as He is and join our voices with the heavenly host in proclaiming: *"Worthy is the Lamb that was slain to receive power, and riches, and wisdom, and strength, and honour, and glory, and blessing"* **(Revelation 5:12)**.

CHAPTER ELEVEN

THE TRIUMPHANT & ETERNAL LAMB

Revelation 21-22 will culminate our study in the New Jerusalem, where the Lamb reigns as both Temple and Light of the eternal city, demonstrating that God's redemptive plan finds its ultimate expression in the Lamb's eternal glory.

THE TRIUMPHANT AND ETERNAL LAMB

T HE FINAL TWO CHAPTERS of scripture do not simply conclude the biblical narrative; they unveil its glorious and eternal consummation. Here, the scarlet thread of redemption, which we have traced from the blood of Abel's offering to the cross of Christ, finds its fulfillment in the triumphant reign of the Lamb. The Apostle John, having been shown the terrifying arc of God's judgment through the tribulation, the binding of Satan, and the final assize at the Great White Throne, is now granted a vision of the eternal state. It is the glorious climax toward which all of history has been moving: a new heaven, a new earth, and the holy city, New Jerusalem, descending from God, bathed in the everlasting light of the Lamb.

What is most striking in this final portrait of eternity is the **enduring centrality of the Lamb**. He is not a figure who, having accomplished His sacrificial work, recedes into the background. Rather, He remains at the very epicenter of all things. The Lamb who was slain on Calvary is the Lamb who reigns from the throne. The Lamb whose blood purchased the church is the Lamb who receives her as His Bride. The Lamb who was judged in our place is the Lamb who is the light and temple of the New Jerusalem.

This is the final, breathtaking answer to the paradox in **Revelation 5**. The One whose sacrificial suffering made Him worthy to open the seals of judgment is the same One whose glory will be the joy and sustenance of His people forever. In these chapters, every promise finds its fulfillment, every sorrow is finally healed, and the curse that has for so long marred God's creation is banished forever. Here we see not the end of a story, but the beginning of an **unending celebration of the finished work of Jesus Christ**, the Lamb of God who was slain, and who lives and reigns for ever and ever.

THE NEW CREATION

The final act of God's redemptive drama begins with a transformation of the cosmos itself: "*And I saw a new heaven and a new earth: for the first heaven and the first earth were passed away; and there was no more sea*" (**Revelation 21:1**). This is no simple renovation of a fallen world, but a complete and total remaking of the entire cosmic order. The Apostle Peter prophesied that the present creation will be dissolved by fervent heat, after which God will make all things new (**2 Peter 3:10, 12**).

This new creation fulfills Isaiah's ancient promise: *"For, behold, I create new heavens and a new earth: and the former shall not be remembered, nor come into mind"* (**Isaiah 65:17**). Every vestige of sin, every shadow of the curse, and every memory of rebellion will be utterly purged from this renewed existence. It is a staggering thought that the soul saved by grace through the blood of the Lamb will outlast the very heavens and earth we now know.

THE NEW JERUSALEM

Following the universal recreation, John beholds *"the holy city, new Jerusalem, coming down from God out of heaven, prepared as a bride adorned for her husband"* (**Revelation 21:2**). An angel later identifies this city explicitly as *"the bride, the Lamb's wife,"* confirming the intimate and eternal union between Christ and His redeemed Church (**Revelation 21:9–10**).

The city's dimensions are of a scale that defies earthly imagination, forming a perfect cube that measures 12,000 furlongs—approximately 1,500 miles—in its length, width, and height. This cubic shape is a profound echo of the Holy of Holies in the tabernacle and temple (**1 Kings 6:20**), signifying that the entire city is now the dwelling place of God, where His presence is no longer veiled but is fully and freely accessible to all the redeemed.

The very structure of the city declares the unity of God's people throughout the ages. Its twelve gates bear the names of the twelve tribes of Israel, while its twelve foundations are inscribed with the names of the twelve apostles of the Lamb. This architecture demonstrates that Old Testament and New Testament saints, though distinct in God's dispensational program, are brought together as one family through the singular, eternal work of the Lamb of God.

THE TABERNACLE OF GOD WITH MEN

From the throne of God, a great voice proclaims the central reality of the eternal state: *"Behold, the tabernacle of God is with men, and he will dwell with them, and they shall be his people, and God himself shall be with them, and be their God"* (**Revelation 21:3**). This is perhaps the most wondrous declaration in all of scripture, for it announces the complete and final fulfillment of God's most cherished covenant promise, a promise woven through the entire fabric of the Bible. It is the end of all distance and the consummation of all desire—God and His redeemed people dwelling together in unhindered, everlasting fellowship.

The word *"tabernacle"* is deliberately chosen. It hearkens back to the temporary dwelling place God established among the Israelites in the wilderness—a tent where His glory was veiled and His presence restricted. It then points to the incarnation, when the Apostle John declared that the Word *"dwelt among us"* (**John 1:14**), literally *"tabernacled"* in human flesh. Now, in the eternal city, that which was temporary and veiled becomes permanent and gloriously manifest. The great longing of God to dwell with His people, a longing that drove the entire plan of redemption, is finally and perfectly realized.

The manifest presence of God and the Lamb becomes the agent of eternal restoration, eradicating every last consequence of the fall. The voice from heaven continues with a series of promises that reverse the curse of **Genesis** with breathtaking finality :

"God shall wipe away all tears from their eyes": This is not only the absence of sorrow, but the active, tender ministration of God Himself. Every tear shed in a fallen world—born of grief, pain, or trial—is personally and permanently wiped away by the hand of the Father.

"there shall be no more death": The final enemy, which has reigned with terror since Adam's sin, is utterly vanquished. The sting of death is removed, the grave has lost its victory, and the redeemed will live in the unending life of God.

"neither sorrow, nor crying, neither shall there be any more pain": These are the bitter fruits of a world groaning under the weight of sin. In the New Jerusalem, every source of anguish—physical, emotional, and spiritual—is removed forever. The very possibility of pain is abolished in the presence of God's perfect peace.

"for the former things are passed away": This is a declaration of total cosmic renewal. The old order, with its cycle of decay, suffering, and death, is not simply improved but completely and eternally replaced by the glory of the new creation.

This final state of blessedness is secured by the triumphant declaration of **Revelation 22:3**: *"there shall be no more curse."* The original curse pronounced in the Garden of Eden—which brought thorns and thistles to the ground, sorrow to childbirth, sweat to labor, and death to man—is utterly and eternally abolished. The work of the Lamb on the cross was not a partial repair but a complete reversal. He who was *"made a curse for us"* (**Galatians 3:13**) has, by His sacrifice, removed the curse forever, ushering in a state of blessing so profound and unending that it surpasses our highest imagination.

THE THRONE OF GOD AND OF THE LAMB

At the very center of the New Jerusalem stands not one throne, but the single *"throne of God and of the Lamb"* (**Revelation 22:1, 3**). This shared throne is a declaration of both the unity and distinction between the Father and the Son, confirming the absolute deity of the Lamb and His rightful place of authority for all eternity.

From this throne proceeds *"a pure river of water of life, clear as crystal"* (**Revelation 22:1**). This river symbolizes the unending, life-giving power that flows from God and the Lamb, recalling both Ezekiel's vision of the temple river and the Lord's own promise of living water. Its perfect clarity speaks of the absolute purity of the life that sustains the saints in glory.

THE LIGHT AND TEMPLE OF THE CITY

In the eternal state, the forms and shadows of earthly worship give way to an unmediated reality. John records, *"And I saw no temple therein: for the Lord God Almighty and the Lamb are the temple of it"* (**Revelation 21:22**). Worship is no longer directed toward a place consecrated by God's presence; rather, it flows directly to God and the Lamb, who have become the living center of all adoration.

Furthermore, the city has no need of created light sources, *"for the glory of God did lighten it, and the Lamb is the light thereof"* (**Revelation 21:23**). The Lamb, once sacrificed to bear the darkness of the world's sin, now illuminates the eternal city with the unending brightness of His own glory, fulfilling Isaiah's prophecy that *"the LORD shall be unto thee an everlasting light"* (**Isaiah 60:19**).

THE RIVER AND TREE OF LIFE

The eternal state is one of endless, sustaining grace, beautifully pictured in the imagery of **Revelation 22:1–2**. Alongside the river of life stands the tree of life, which was first seen in the Garden of Eden and now reappears in the New Jerusalem. Its presence signifies that God's people have been restored to full and everlasting fellowship with Him. The tree yields twelve manner of fruits, a new crop each month, suggesting the infinite variety and richness of eternal existence.

The leaves of the tree are for the *"healing of the nations,"* a phrase that does not imply the presence of sickness, but rather speaks of the perpetual state of wholeness and restoration that God's life-giving provision maintains for all eternity.

FACE-TO-FACE WITH THE LAMB

In what is surely among the most precious and profound promises in all of scripture, the Apostle John reveals the pinnacle of the believer's hope: *"And they shall see his face; and his name shall be in their foreheads"* (**Revelation 22:4**). This is the ultimate fulfillment of the deepest longing of every redeemed soul. Since the fall of man in the Garden of Eden, a veil has separated man from the unveiled glory of God. Even Moses, with whom God spoke *"face to face, as a man speaketh unto his friend"* (**Exodus 33:11**), was denied the sight of God's full glory, for God declared, *"Thou canst not see my face: for there shall no man see me, and live"* (**Exodus 33:20**).

What was impossible for fallen man, even for the greatest of the prophets, becomes the everlasting joy of the saints in glory. The sin that necessitated the veil has been washed away by the blood of the Lamb, and the redeemed, clothed in the righteousness of Christ, are now able to stand in the unmediated presence of the Holy God and gaze upon His face without fear. We will see the face of the One who spoke worlds into existence and the face of the Lamb who was slain for us—the very face that was once marred more than any man's (**Isaiah 52:14**) will be the source of our eternal delight. This is the essence of heaven: not streets of gold or pearly gates, but unhindered, **face-to-face communion with the God who loved us and gave Himself for us**.

Paired with this beatific vision is the promise that *"his name shall be in their foreheads."* This is far more than identification; it is a mark of eternal security, godly ownership, and perfect intimacy. In the dark days of the tribulation, the ungodly were sealed with the mark of the beast, a sign of their allegiance to Satan and their ultimate damnation. In glorious contrast, the redeemed will bear the name of their God and of the Lamb upon their foreheads, a visible and eternal declaration of to whom they belong.

This divine seal signifies:

Ownership: We are His, purchased by the precious blood of the Lamb.

Protection: We are eternally secure under His care.

Identification: We are perfectly conformed to His character, bearing His family name for all to see.

Honor: It is the highest possible honor, signifying our status as the Bride of the Lamb and co-heirs of His eternal kingdom.

To see His face is the consummation of our worship; to bear His name is the consummation of our identity. Together, they represent the complete restoration of all that was lost in the fall and the fulfillment of every promise God has ever made to His people.

ETERNAL SERVICE AND REIGN

The final verses of Holy Scripture reveal the eternal occupation of the redeemed, and it is a glorious paradox of humble service and royal authority. The saints, standing in the unmediated light of the Lamb, are called His servants who *"shall serve him,"* and yet in the very same breath it is declared that *"they shall reign for ever and ever"* (**Revelation 22:3, 5**). In this, the redeemed are brought into the final and most perfect conformity to their Savior, following the pattern of the Lamb Himself, who took upon Him the form of a servant, and is now exalted as King of kings and Lord of lords.

This is not the burdensome toil of a fallen world, marked by sweat and fatigue. This is the service of unhindered worship, the glad and willing activity of glorified beings whose greatest delight is to execute the perfect will of their King. **As priests**, the saints will have the everlasting privilege of direct access to the very throne of God, offering up a ceaseless tribute of praise and adoration. **As kings**, they will share in the Lamb's eternal dominion, exercising the authority He has delegated to them in the administration of His kingdom. The scepter of our reign will be the very instrument of our service; our highest authority will be our perfect submission to His.

Here, at the close of God's final revelation, the doctrine of the Lamb of God finds its perfect and glorious consummation. The scarlet thread that began with the coats of skins at the gate of a lost Eden—a thread traced through the blood of Abel's offering, the ram provided for Isaac on Moriah, the Passover lamb in Egypt, the intricate sacrifices of the Levitical law, the prophetic portrait of Isaiah's suffering servant, and the historical reality of Calvary's cross—is now woven into the eternal tapestry of the New Jerusalem. The Lamb who was slain has triumphed over sin, death, and hell, and His redeemed people, purchased by His blood and sealed with His name, will now share in His glory, His service, and His reign for ever and ever.

The story that began with a sacrifice ends with a throne. The Victim has become the Victor, and His victory is ours. To Him who loved us, and washed us from our sins in His own blood, and hath made us kings and priests unto God and his Father; to him be glory and dominion for ever and ever. Amen.

CHAPTER TWELVE

PROGRESS OF THE DOCTRINE OF THE LAMB

THE UNFOLDING GLORY OF THE LAMB

WITHIN THE SACRED LIBRARY of Holy Scripture, there runs a single, unifying theme of such brilliance and power that all other doctrines find their place in relation to it. It is the scarlet thread of redemption, the grand, unfolding revelation of the Lamb of God. This is no static concept, but a truth that God has graciously unveiled in stages, a doctrine that progresses from the shadows of **Genesis** to the unclouded glory of **Revelation**. To trace this progression is to witness the very heart of God's redemptive plan being laid bare, providing not only unshakeable doctrinal certainty but also a holy fire to compel our own testimony of the One *"which taketh away the sin of the world"* (**John 1:29**).

THE ORIGIN OF THE LAMB CONCEPT IN GENESIS

The first notes of this concept are heard in the earliest days of human history, in a world freshly marred by sin. In **Genesis 4**, we find Abel approaching God, not with the fruit of the cursed ground which his brother Cain profanely offered, but with *"the firstlings of his flock and of the fat thereof."* The LORD had respect unto Abel's offering, and **He-**

brews 11:4 illuminates the reason: *"By faith Abel offered unto God a more excellent sacrifice than Cain."*

But whence came this faith? From what prior revelation did Abel learn that blood must be shed? The answer lies at the gate of a lost Paradise. After Adam and Eve's transgression, when they stood shivering in the shame of their own fig-leaf righteousness, it was the LORD God Himself who acted. In an act of profound mercy, He made for them *"coats of skins, and clothed them"* (**Genesis 3:21**). An innocent life was taken, its blood was shed, and its skin provided a covering for their naked guilt. In this singular act, God established an eternal principle: **access to His holy presence requires the shedding of innocent blood**. Abel's offering was an act of obedient faith, a confession that only a God appointed substitute could atone for sin and satisfy the righteous demands of a holy God.

ABRAHAM AND ISAAC: THE LAMB AS SUBSTITUTION

The doctrine of the Lamb takes a mighty step forward upon the lonely summit of Mount Moriah. Here, in the crucible of faith described in **Genesis 22**, the principle of sacrifice is deepened into the personal reality of substitution. As Abraham and his beloved son journey toward the place of offering, Isaac's innocent question pierces the heart: *"Behold the fire and the wood: but where is the lamb for a burnt offering?"* (**Genesis 22:7**). Abraham's reply is not one of despair, but of magnificent, prophetic faith: *"My son, God will provide himself a lamb for a burnt offering"* (**Genesis 22:8**).

As the heart-rending narrative reaches its climax, the knife is raised. At that precise moment, the voice of God stays the father's hand. Then,

"Abraham lifted up his eyes, and looked, and behold behind him a ram caught in a thicket by his horns: and Abraham went and took the ram, and offered him up for a burnt offering in the stead of his son" (**Genesis 22:13**). The phrase is monumental: *in the stead of.* The ram, provided by God, dies so that Isaac might live. This is the doctrine of substitution in living color. The imagery is rich with prophetic meaning: **the ram caught in a thicket by its horns, a faint shadow of the crown of thorns that would one day encircle our Saviour's brow; the location itself, Mount Moriah, the very region where Jerusalem would stand and Christ would be crucified**. God was teaching His people that the Lamb would serve as a substitute, taking the place of condemned sinners.

THE PASSOVER LAMB: COVERING AND DELIVERANCE

In the dark and terrible night of God's judgment upon Egypt, the revelation of the Lamb's work expands dramatically. The institution of the Passover in **Exodus 12** reveals a Lamb whose blood provides not only individual covering but also national deliverance. Each household in Israel was commanded to take *"a lamb without blemish, a male of the first year"* (**Exodus 12:5**), slay it, and apply its blood to the two side posts and the upper door post of their houses.

The promise was absolute: *"And the blood shall be to you for a token upon the houses where ye are: and when I see the blood, I will pass over you, and the plague shall not be upon you to destroy you, when I smite the land of Egypt"* (**Exodus 12:13**). The lesson is stark and eternal: **when the judgment of God falls, no human merit or effort can avail; safety is found only beneath the covering of the shed blood of the lamb**. The scope of the Lamb's work has now widened from a single man to an entire family, and by extension, a whole nation. Furthermore, the lamb here accomplishes not only pardon from death but also deliverance from bondage, foreshadowing Christ, our Passover, who redeems us from the bondage of sin.

THE DAY OF ATONEMENT: NATIONAL CLEANSING

In the solemn ceremonies of **Leviticus 16**, God adds further depth to His progressive revelation. On the Day of Atonement, though goats were the appointed animals, the principles they embodied are central to understanding the work of Christ as the Lamb of God. Two goats were chosen. One was slain *"for the LORD"* as a sin offering, its blood carried by the high priest into the Holy of Holies to make atonement, satisfying God's justice. This represents propitiation.

The second goat, the scapegoat, had the sins of the entire nation confessed over its head. The high priest would *"lay both his hands upon the head of the live goat, and confess over him all the iniquities of the children of Israel... putting them upon the head of the goat, and shall send him away... into the wilderness"* (**Leviticus 16:21**). This goat, bearing the imputed sin of the people, was led away to a place of separation, never to return. This represents the complete removal of sin—atonement. Together, these two goats provide a magnificent, composite picture of the finished work of Christ, who both satisfies God's wrath against sin and removes our transgressions as far as the east is from the west. The efficacy of the sacrifice has now expanded to cover an entire nation.

ISAIAH'S SUFFERING SERVANT: THE LAMB AS A PERSON

For centuries, the truth of the Lamb was taught through the silent, bleeding ministry of animal sacrifices. But in the sublime prophecy of **Isaiah 53**, the Lamb steps out of the shadows of type and ritual and is revealed as a Person. The prophet, gazing with Spirit-anointed eyes across the ages, beholds One who "*is brought as a lamb to the slaughter, and as a sheep before her shearers is dumb, so he openeth not his mouth*" (**Isaiah 53:7**).

This is no animal. This is a willing, suffering Servant who personally bears our griefs, carries our sorrows, is wounded for our transgressions, and bruised for our iniquities. The Lamb is now identified as a conscious substitute who provides propitiation through His own person. With this clearer focus comes another expansion of scope. This Servant shall justify "*many*" (**Isaiah 53:11**), bearing their iniquities. The work of the Lamb is beginning to look beyond the borders of Israel to embrace a wider harvest of souls.

JOHN THE BAPTIST'S TESTIMONY: THE LAMB WHO TAKES AWAY SIN

All the streams of Old Testament prophecy and type converge in a single, glorious moment on the banks of the Jordan River. As John the Baptist sees Jesus of Nazareth approaching, he makes the declaration that serves as the pivot-point of all redemptive history: "*Behold the Lamb of God, which taketh away the sin of the world!*" (**John 1:29**).

Consider the magnificent fullness of this statement:

First, He is *the* Lamb of God—not just another sacrifice, but the unique, ultimate Lamb prophesied by Abraham.

Second, this Lamb *"taketh away"* sin—He does not only cover it for a time, as the blood of bulls and goats did, but He removes it completely and forever. As **Hebrews 10:4** affirms, *"it is not possible that the blood of bulls and of goats should take away sins."* Only God's Lamb can do that.

Third, He takes away the sin *"of the world"*—the scope has now reached its fullest extent. The provision is not for one man, one family, or one nation, but for all humanity. Salvation is now opened to whosoever in the world will believe.

THE ETHIOPIAN EUNUCH: INDIVIDUAL APPLICATION THROUGH FAITH

The glorious, objective work of the Lamb becomes a subjective, personal reality through faith, as powerfully illustrated in **Acts 8**. Philip the evangelist is guided to a man of Ethiopia, a eunuch of great authority, returning from a fruitless journey to worship at Jerusalem. He is reading from **Isaiah 53**, perplexed by the identity of the suffering Lamb. Beginning at that very scripture, Philip *"preached unto him Jesus."*

The result was immediate and transformative. The man believed and was saved. This account demonstrates the very purpose of all progressive revelation: **it is meant to lead a seeking soul to a personal encounter with the living Christ**. The Law and the Prophets had done their preparatory work, creating a thirst that only the Lamb of God could quench. What the eunuch could not find in the rituals of the Temple, he found in a moment through simple faith in Jesus Christ. The work of the Lamb becomes effectual in a life the instant it is believed.

PETER'S DECLARATION: FULL REDEMPTION IN THE LAMB

The apostle Peter, in his first epistle, provides one of the most comprehensive summaries of our redemption in the Lamb. He writes: "*Forasmuch as ye know that ye were not redeemed with corruptible things, as silver and gold... But with the precious blood of Christ, as of a lamb without blemish and without spot: Who verily was foreordained before the foundation of the world, but was manifest in these last times for you*" (**1 Peter 1:18-20**).

Peter's words establish several foundational pillars of our faith. Our redemption was purchased by a price of infinite value: the "*precious blood of Christ.*" The Redeemer Himself is the perfect, spotless Lamb. This plan of redemption was no rushed afterthought; it was "*foreordained before the foundation of the world.*" God's Lamb was chosen in eternity past for a sacrifice that would be made manifest in time for our sakes. This passage shows that the Lamb provides a full and final redemption, a comprehensive salvation that is the believer's possession from the moment of faith.

THE TRIUMPHANT LAMB IN REVELATION

The final book of the Bible pulls back the veil and shows us the Lamb in His ultimate glory. The progression is breathtaking. The Lamb who was offered in sacrifice by Abel, who was provided as a substitute for Isaac, who was slain for the deliverance of Israel, and who was crucified on Calvary, is now seen standing in the very midst of heaven's throne. John writes, "*And I beheld, and, lo, in the midst of the throne... stood a Lamb as it had been slain*" (**Revelation 5:6**).

The marks of His sacrificial death are upon Him for all eternity, a perpetual reminder of the price He paid. Yet this slain Lamb is also the Lion of the tribe of Judah, the conquering King. All of heaven erupts in worship before Him: *"Worthy is the Lamb that was slain to receive power, and riches, and wisdom, and strength, and honour, and glory, and blessing"* (**Revelation 5:12**). The victim has become the victor; the sacrifice is now the King. The Lamb who died for our sins now reigns in ineffable glory, and in the eternal city, the Lord God Almighty and the Lamb are its temple and its light (**Revelation 21:22**). What began with a single sacrifice in **Genesis** finds its glorious and eternal consummation in the worship of the Triumphant Lamb forever.

THE PROGRESSIVE EXPANSION OF THE LAMB'S WORK

As we have journeyed through the scripture, the magnificent, God ordered progression of this doctrine has become clear. God has gradually widened the lens, revealing ever more of the Lamb's glory and the scope of His work:

A lamb for sin (Genesis 4): Establishing the foundational principle of blood atonement.

A lamb for an individual person (Genesis 22): Revealing the core truth of substitution.

A lamb for a family (Exodus 12): Providing corporate protection and deliverance.

A lamb for a nation (Leviticus 16): Effecting national cleansing and atonement.

A lamb for many (Isaiah 53): Expanding the sacrificial work beyond national Israel.

A Lamb for the world (John 1): Opening salvation to whosoever will believe.

A Lamb for all time (1 Peter 1): Spanning from eternity past to eternity future.

A Lamb for the throne (Revelation 5): Reigning in glory as the object of all worship.

A Lamb for eternity (Revelation 21-22): Dwelling with His people as their everlasting light and joy.

This beautiful progression demonstrates God's masterful plan, with each stage building upon and fulfilling what came before, until the full glory of Christ, the Lamb slain from the foundation of the world, is revealed.

OUR RESPONSE: TESTIFYING OF THE LAMB

What shall be our response to such a staggering revelation? The word of God gives us our mandate: *"And they overcame him by the blood of the Lamb, and by the word of their testimony; and they loved not their lives unto the death"* (**Revelation 12:11**). Victory in the Christian life is inextricably linked to the blood of the Lamb and our faithful testimony concerning Him.

The Bible is God's testimony of His Lamb, and our lives are to be a living echo of that same testimony. How can we, who have been cleansed by His precious blood, who have the indwelling Holy Spirit as our power, and who possess the perfect word of God in the King James Bible, remain silent? How can a day pass wherein we do not speak of the One who loved us and gave Himself for us? It is a grievous concern in our day that so many who profess salvation are silent witnesses. In the New Testament, salvation was almost invariably followed by testimony. The doctrine of the Lamb, when truly grasped by the soul, is not a matter for quiet contemplation alone; it is a fire in the bones, a holy compulsion to tell a lost and dying world about the Saviour.

THE COMPLETE WORK OF THE LAMB

From the first blood sacrifice in the shadow of Eden to the triumphant Lamb upon heaven's throne, scripture is the revelation of redemption through the Lamb. Each passage we have visited has added another layer of understanding, not contradicting what came before, but fulfilling and clarifying it. This is the method of progressive revelation: **earlier truths are not discarded but are brought to their glorious and intended fullness in the person and work of Jesus Christ.**

He is our propitiation, our substitute, our covering, and our atonement. His blood purchased our full redemption, and His resurrection is the guarantee of our eternal glory with Him. Let us therefore testify with holy boldness of this Lamb. Let us proclaim His finished work to a world that desperately needs to hear that there is a Lamb who takes away sin. And let us live in eager anticipation of that day when we shall join the heavenly choir, crying with a loud voice, *"Worthy is the Lamb that was slain!"*

From the promise of the seed of the woman in **Genesis**, through Abel's sacrifice, Abraham's obedience, the Passover's protection, Leviticus's rituals, Isaiah's prophecy, John's proclamation, and the apostles' testimony—all finds its eternal consummation in the triumphant Lamb. The One who was slain is now upon the throne, and of His kingdom there shall be no end. What manner of love is this, that we should not only be saved by Him, but be called the bride of the Lamb and joint-heirs with Him in His eternal kingdom! May this glorious truth kindle in our hearts an unquenchable flame of devotion to Him who has bought us for Himself, that we might share in His glory forever.

CHAPTER THIRTEEN

THE LAMB OF GOD, YOUR ONLY HOPE

FRIEND, THIS MESSAGE IS FOR YOU.

A T THIS POINT IN our study, I must ask for a moment of your most earnest attention. It may be that you have come to these concluding words as a curious traveler, having journeyed through the doctrinal details of this book with a mind that is interested but a heart that remains untouched. Or perhaps you are a soul in flight, and heaven itself has guided you to these pages, bringing you to a solemn and decisive pause.

Whatever the path that led you here, the Lord has something of eternal weight to say to you concerning the Lamb of God, who was slain for your sins. All that has been written, all the mighty truths of sacrifice and redemption that have marched across these pages, now converge upon a single, piercing question directed at you.

For there is but one Lamb, and one sacrifice, that can lift the burden of sin from a human soul and open the gates to everlasting life. His name is Jesus Christ. This is not a doctrine to be examined, but a Person to be received. And it is my most fervent prayer that you will not put this book down without entrusting yourself wholly to Him.

YOUR SOUL'S GREAT NEED OF THE LAMB

If we are to find the remedy, we must first be honest about the disease. And so, I must ask you to look with me, for a moment, into the mirror of God's holy word to understand our true spiritual condition. The scripture, which cannot err, declares with solemn certainty, "*For all have sinned, and come short of the glory of God*" (**Romans 3:23**). This is not a charge against the notoriously wicked alone; it is a description of every human heart. We may measure ourselves against our neighbors and find some comfort, we may be diligent in our religious duties, and our lives may be filled with charitable works. But when we stand our character against the blazing holiness of God, we see how far we have fallen short of His perfect standard.

The word of God speaks plainly about the consequence of this condition: "*the wages of sin is death*" (**Romans 6:23**). This is a wage that is truly earned. It is more than the cessation of breath; it is a spiritual separation from the God of all life and light. As the prophet **Isaiah** so vividly described it, "*your iniquities have separated between you and your God, and your sins have hid his face from you*" (**Isaiah 59:2**). Imagine a vast and impassable chasm opened between your soul and the God who created you for fellowship with Himself. Such is the gulf that sin has fixed, and no bridge of human effort can ever span it.

Perhaps you feel in your heart, "*But my faults are small. I have done no great evil.*" Friend, let us listen carefully to the Lord Himself. God's standard is not the shifting line of human comparison, but the unbending rule of His own perfection. Our Lord Jesus said, "*Be ye therefore perfect, even as your Father which is in heaven is perfect*" (**Matthew 5:48**). Have we ever spoken a word that was not entirely true? Have we ever harbored an unkind thought? If so, we have transgressed His holy law, and the scripture warns that *"whosoever shall keep the whole law, and yet offend in one point, he is guilty of all"* (**James 2:10**). A single crack can shatter the finest vase.

It is a humbling truth, but our best efforts cannot save us. The prophet **Isaiah** tells us again that in God's pure sight, even *"all our righteousnesses are as filthy rags"* (**Isaiah 64:6**). The most devout church attendance, the most solemn baptism, the most earnest religious activity—none of these can cleanse the soul or pay the debt that sin has incurred. For this, you need something far greater. You need God's remedy. **You need the precious blood of the Lamb.**

THE UNCHANGING TESTIMONY OF THE BLOOD

From the moment sin first cast its long and sorrowful shadow across human history, God Himself began to teach a profound and unchanging lesson. It is a truth written in scarlet from the very gates of a lost Eden: that the path back to fellowship with a holy God is a path that must be consecrated by the shedding of innocent blood.

Consider Adam and Eve, standing in the chill of their newfound shame. Their own efforts—the flimsy aprons of fig leaves—could not cover their guilt. And so, in an act of breathtaking mercy, it was the LORD God who drew near. He did not offer a word of instruction alone; He performed an act of revelation. An innocent life was taken, its blood was shed, and its skin provided a covering for their nakedness. This was the first sacrifice, an object lesson in substitution. Here, at the dawn of our fallen race, God Himself established the solemn principle: an innocent must suffer for the guilty to be covered.

This was the truth Abel embraced by faith. When he brought *"the firstlings of his flock"* as his offering, he was not performing a religious duty; he was confessing his agreement with God's revealed way. The Lord had respect unto his sacrifice because it was a testimony to the necessity of a substitute. Cain's offering, though the product of his own honest toil, was rejected because it was a tragic declaration of self-sufficiency. It was an attempt to approach God on his own terms, ignoring the lesson that had already been taught.

This crimson thread is woven throughout all the ages that follow. We see it on the lonely peak of Mount Moriah, where God provided a ram to die in the place of Isaac. We feel its protective power on the dark night of Passover in Egypt, where the blood of a lamb on the doorpost was the sole defense against the angel of death. We witness its necessity year after year in the solemn rites of the Day of Atonement, as the high priest entered the awful holiness of God's presence, never without blood, to make atonement for the sins of the people.

Yet, as the writer to the **Hebrews** reminds us, these were but shadows and figures. They were precious and God-given reminders, but they were temporary. *"For it is not possible that the blood of bulls and of goats should take away sins"* (**Hebrews 10:4**). Every one of these sacrifices, from Abel's lamb onward, was a signpost pointing down the corridor of time to the one, final, perfect sacrifice that was to come—the true Lamb of God, Jesus Christ.

JESUS CHRIST: THE LAMB GOD HAS PROVIDED

All the streams of prophecy, all the shadows of sacrifice, which had flowed through the long centuries, met in one glorious, history-altering moment. On the banks of the Jordan River, John the Baptist, the last of the old prophets, saw Jesus of Nazareth approaching. With a voice ringing with the certainty of heaven, he cried, *"Behold the Lamb of God, which taketh away the sin of the world!"* (**John 1:29**). This was not simply another lamb in a long line of sacrifices; this was **the** Lamb, the one to whom all others pointed. This was God's own Son, stepping out of eternity and into time, for the express purpose of dying for sinners.

To be the sacrifice our souls required, this Lamb had to be perfect. And He was. The Apostle Peter, who walked with Him and knew Him, would later write that we are redeemed by the precious blood of Christ, *"as of a lamb without blemish and without spot"* (**1 Peter 1:19**). He lived a life of such flawless purity that He alone fulfilled every righteous requirement of God's holy law. Though He was tempted in all points just as we are, He remained *"yet without sin"* (**Hebrews 4:15**). In Him, there was no stain, no defect, no shadow of turning.

It was this perfect, sinless Son of God who went to the cross and died for you. The prophet **Isaiah**, gazing with Spirit-anointed eyes across seven hundred years, saw this very scene and wrote of it with heartbreaking clarity: *"But he was wounded for our transgressions, he was bruised for our iniquities: the chastisement of our peace was upon him; and with his stripes we are healed. All we like sheep have gone astray; we have turned every one to his own way; and the LORD hath laid on him the iniquity of us all"* (**Isaiah 53:5-6**).

Do you see the glorious transaction? On that cross, Jesus became your substitute. He willingly gathered up your sins, your guilt, your shame, and your condemnation, and took them all upon Himself. God the Father, in His unswerving justice, poured out upon His own beloved

Son the full measure of wrath that your sins and my sins deserved, so that He might, in perfect righteousness, show mercy to you.

And lest there be any doubt that this sacrifice was sufficient and accepted, three days later, **God raised Him from the dead**. The resurrection is God's eternal *"Amen!"* to the finished work of Christ. It is the triumphant proof that sin has been atoned for, that death has been defeated, and that hell has been conquered. The tomb is empty! The Lamb that was slain is alive for evermore, holding in His hand access to life and hope for all who will trust in Him.

IN THIS LAMB IS YOUR ONLY HOPE

Friend, having considered the greatness of our need and the perfection of God's provision, we are brought to a most solemn and necessary conclusion. I must speak it plainly, for love requires clarity in matters of eternal destiny: **Jesus Christ is the only hope for the salvation of your soul**.

This is no narrow opinion of man, but the clear, shining testimony of God's own word. The Lord Jesus Himself, who is the very embodiment of truth, made this gracious declaration: *"I am the way, the truth, and the life: no man cometh unto the Father, but by me"* (**John 14:6**). He did not present Himself as one of many paths, but as the single, God-appointed Way. The apostle Peter, filled with the Holy Ghost, echoed this same certainty when he proclaimed, *"Neither is there salvation in any other: for there is none other name under heaven given among men, whereby we must be saved"* (**Acts 4:12**). God has not scattered our hope among many saviors; **He has concentrated it all in the person of His beloved Son**.

Therefore, we must gently but firmly set aside any other trust.

We cannot be saved by our **good works**, for scripture says, "*Not by works of righteousness which we have done, but according to his mercy he saved us*" (**Titus 3:5**). Salvation is a gift of mercy, not a wage for service.

We cannot be saved by our **religious duties**, for "*a man is not justified by the works of the law, but by the faith of Jesus Christ*" (**Galatians 2:16**). Rituals can never cleanse the deep stain of sin.

We cannot be saved by our **church affiliation**, for our Lord taught, "*Except a man be born again, he cannot see the kingdom of God*" (**John 3:3**). It is a new life from God, not a new name on a roll, that is required.

We cannot be saved by our own **personal goodness**, for when God looks at the heart, He finds, "*There is none that doeth good, no, not one*" (**Romans 3:12**).

Every door that we might try to open to God on our own strength is barred. There is but one door, and it is the Lamb Himself. The precious blood of the Lamb is the only payment God will ever accept for the debt of your sin.

TRUST THIS LAMB FOR SALVATION

We come now to the most vital and blessed question that a human soul can ever ask: How can I be saved? How can I, a sinner, be made right with a holy God? The answer, I am overjoyed to tell you, is not found in a complex series of tasks, but in a simple and profound act of faith. The way to God is not a ladder we must climb, **but a gift we must receive.**

The Apostle Paul states it with beautiful clarity: "*That if thou shalt confess with thy mouth the Lord Jesus, and shalt believe in thine heart that God hath raised him from the dead, thou shalt be saved*" (**Romans 10:9**).

Salvation is a matter of entrusting yourself completely—your sin, your soul, your eternal future—into the loving hands of Jesus Christ, **resting wholly upon His finished work on the cross**.

This saving faith is composed of three simple, yet profound, elements:

It begins with an honest **admission** before God that you are a sinner, and that you stand in need of His mercy. It is the cry of the heart that says, *"God, I am what your word says I am, and I can do nothing to save myself."*

It rests upon a confident **belief** in the truth of the gospel: that Jesus Christ, the Son of God, died for your specific sins, that He was buried, and that He rose again the third day, just as the scriptures promised (**1 Corinthians 15:1–4**). This is not a vague hope, but a faith founded on a historical fact.

It is expressed by **calling** upon Him. It is turning from all other trusts and, in the quiet sanctuary of your heart, calling on the name of the Lord for the salvation of your soul (**Romans 10:9-10**). The promise is *"whosoever shall call upon the name of the Lord shall be saved"* (**Romans 10:13**).

Friend, please see that this is more than just a mental agreement that Jesus existed. The devils themselves believe that, and they tremble, but no reconciliation is offered them. Saving faith is to cast yourself upon Him as your only hope, to trust Him personally as the one who died for *your* sins and rose again for *your* justification. It is to rest in Him as your Lamb.

The Urgency of This Moment

And so, my friend, I must speak to your heart with a pressing and solemn urgency. This moment, while you read these words and the Spirit of God ministers to your soul, is a holy and precious opportunity. The Bible does not point us to a more convenient season, but declares with profound significance, *"behold, now is the accepted time; behold, now is the day of salvation"* (**2 Corinthians 6:2**). We are given no promise of tomorrow. As the wise man cautions, *"Boast not thyself of to morrow; for thou knowest not what a day may bring forth"* (**Proverbs 27:1**). The invitation of grace is extended to you *today*.

I plead with you, do not turn away from the One who speaks. The Bible warns that a heart can become hardened through continued refusal. When God's voice calls, we are implored, *"To day if ye will hear his voice, harden not your hearts"* (**Hebrews 3:15**). Each time the gentle call of Jesus is ignored, the spiritual ear grows a little more dull, and the heart becomes a little less tender to His love. Do not let that tragedy befall you.

The Glorious Inheritance of Faith

Should you, in this moment, genuinely entrust yourself to Jesus Christ as your Saviour, several wonderful and immediate realities become yours.

This is not a gradual process, but a miraculous, instantaneous inheritance bestowed by grace:

You are utterly Forgiven. The crushing weight of your sin is lifted, the entire debt is cancelled. In Christ, *"we have redemption through his blood, the forgiveness of sins"* (**Ephesians 1:7**). Every transgression is washed away, remembered no more against you forever.

You are fully Justified. You are not only pardoned, but declared right-eous in the sight of God, clothed in the very perfection of Christ Himself. Because of this, you now have *"peace with God through our Lord Jesus Christ"* (**Romans 5:1**). The enmity is over; you are brought near as a beloved child.

You possess Eternal Life. This is not just a promise of living for a long time, but the impartation of a new quality of life—the very life of God in your soul. *"For God so loved the world, that he gave his only begotten Son, that whosoever believeth in him should not perish, but have everlasting life"* (**John 3:16**).

You are made a New Creature. The moment you believe, a divine miracle takes place. *"Therefore if any man be in Christ, he is a new creature: old things are passed away; behold, all things are become new"* (**2 Corinthians 5:17**). You are born again from above.

You are Sealed by the Holy Spirit. From the instant of your faith, the Spirit of God comes to dwell within you, marking you as God's own treasured possession, kept secure unto the day of redemption (**Ephesians 1:13-14**).

WILL YOU TRUST THE LAMB?

The Lamb of God, in His infinite love and patience, is calling to you now. He says, *"Behold, I stand at the door, and knock: if any man hear my voice, and open the door, I will come in to him"* (**Revelation 3:20**). He is knocking at the door of your heart. He is not asking you to first make yourself worthy, to clean the house of your soul before He will enter. He is asking only that you would open the door and let Him in, just as you are. He desires to save you, to cleanse you, and to have fellowship with you.

One day, you will see this Lamb face to face. If you have trusted in Him, you will join that mighty chorus of the redeemed, singing with unspeakable joy, "*Worthy is the Lamb that was slain to receive power, and riches, and wisdom, and strength, and honour, and glory, and blessing*" (**Revelation 5:12**). But if you turn from His gracious offer, you will face Him still, not as a Saviour, but as your righteous Judge.

The choice, in this sacred moment, is yours. The Lamb of God has done everything necessary for your salvation, I pray you choose wisely!

In Memoriam: A Dedication to Charlie Kirk

It is with a heavy heart and profound sorrow that this work must now bear a dedication born of tragedy. This book is dedicated to the memory of Charlie Kirk, a voice silenced in its prime, whose earthly labors were brought to a sudden and violent end.

Mr. Kirk was a man who, with youthful vigor and unwavering resolve, took his stand for Jesus Christ in the public square. He did not shrink from the contention of our age but entered the arena with a clarion call to the truths he held dear. He bore the reproach of the cross with a boldness that challenged the prevailing spirit of the times, and for this, he was both admired and assailed.

That such a voice could be so cruelly extinguished is a grievous testament to the spiritual malady that afflicts our nation. A shadow has fallen upon our land, where, in a moment of careless and heartless violence, a wife is made a widow and children are left fatherless. What a sad and somber reality of our age, that a home should be so broken, and the most sacred of earthly bonds torn asunder by the hand of another. This lamentable act is a sorrowful signpost, pointing to a people who have lost their way and are wandering in a darkness of their own making.

In the face of this dark sorrow, the central truth of this humble book shines with a more urgent and piercing light. The discord and strife that plague our world are but the symptoms of a heart separated from its Creator. The turmoil in our streets is a reflection of the turmoil in the soul. And so, now more than ever, we must proclaim the eternal remedy. When the voices of men are silenced and the foundations of society tremble, Jesus is still the answer.

THE LAMB OF GOD

May the memory of this brother serve not to incite bitterness, but to ignite in us a renewed passion to point a lost and hurting world to the Lamb of God, who alone taketh away the sin of the world. He is our only hope, our enduring peace, and our everlasting light.